VIBRATIONS

Vibrations

Based on the Edgar Cayce Readings

by J. Everett Irion

A.R.E.® PRESS • VIRGINIA BEACH • VIRGINIA

4th Printing, June 1985

ISBN 87604-120-9

Printed in the U.S.A.

CONTENTS

Foreword

In this study of vibrations, Everett Irion has accomplished an extraordinary feat. Whereas most writers, lecturers, teachers and researchers deal, in their attempts to be practical, with issues that clearly pertain to everyday life, there is occasionally a rare pioneer who reaches deeper to the very core of reality. These pioneers may not receive their proper recognition quickly because they have moved in their thought beyond the ordinary; it is only later that the true significance of their work is recognized. Then their subject matter, thought at first to be too theoretical, is discovered to be more basic, relevant and applicable than topics previously considered more practical.

A colleague who had written more than 50 books once told me in a moment of profundity, "In science, keep your eye on the energy." All of us are beginning to understand how all that we experience in the earth is a manifestation of energy. However, in our studies and inquiries, we frequently concern ourselves more with phenomena than with the energy and the direction of the energy behind these phenomena. In the present study, which at the same time deals with philosophy, physics and psychology, we are moved from the phenomena of these fields to the nature of the energy behind them. The great advance of modern psychology, called dynamic psychology, has been to recognize the fact that there are energies behind experiences. This book takes us several steps further in investigating the nature of these energies. As we undertake this study, we should accept the author's invitation and focus on the impact of the study in its entirety rather than dwell on problems raised by some of the details. There is, admittedly, much research yet to be done regarding these details. The purpose of this pioneering work is to stake out some major areas of consideration.

Over the years, many people have been challenged, delighted

and, not infrequently, puzzled by the extraordinary mind of Everett Irion. Sometimes we like to read a book by a person whose ideas are the same as our own but who articulates them better than we can express them. On occasion, however, we may also be excited by allowing the mind of another to give us a perspective such as our own mind might never have conceived. We must remember that we are all blind with respect to higher realities, and we should value the reports of those who are touching another part of "the elephant" in the oft-told story of the blind men. In such a case, it is most important that we allow our minds to become quickened rather than diverted by the points at which there may seem to be disagreement.

For readers of this study who are especially interested in the work of Edgar Cayce, it is important to stress that the issues dealt with herein are at the very heart of the basic premises of the philosophy of the Cayce readings. As you begin this book, we challenge you again with one of the passages of Scripture most frequently quoted in the readings: "Study to show thyself approved unto God . . ." (II Timothy 2:15)

Herbert Bruce Puryear, Ph.D.
Research Services Division Director

Introduction

This treatise on vibration is presented as a study. It is intended not to provide the reader with a ready-made formula of what vibrations are and how they can be used, but to put forth certain concepts that will stimulate him to seek his own answers. This paper is meant to be provoking and, it is hoped, enlightening. To be understood, it should be read and reread, and the ideas it presents should be tried out in everyday life. It is realized that some of the concepts it contains will be controversial, especially when read by those better versed in the technical aspects of the subject than this writer. Such controversy is part and parcel of the stimulation hoped for. Some readers may discover that for them the Edgar Cayce material we have used holds meanings not necessarily in line with the ideas presented here, while others may find different readings more appropriate to the various points under consideration; this, too, is part of that desired stimulation.

It should be evident that an in-depth study of vibration would entail far more than the present treatise, but it is hoped that an interim need will be met by this effort. In fact, any one of the concepts we take up could well be the subject of a study much longer than the whole of this one. The reader may therefore feel that some of the ideas considered here are dealt with too briefly, that much more could be said on the topic. On the other hand, it might seem to some that too much is made of other concepts, the paths branching out from them being followed farther than is necessary. In each case the intent was to limit our discussion to the minimum needed for logical continuity, but at the same time to include enough material to indicate the relationships among the ideas presented in the different sections of this work.

Vibration is not only a deep subject, with far-reaching implications; it is a vast one, encompassing mathematical areas such as geometry and optics, the aesthetics of color, such metaphysical considerations as the nature of time and space, and various philosophical and theological concepts. The present study draws upon material from each of these fields, but it treats none of them exhaustively, for any attempt to do so would take us far beyond the range we are able to cover competently. We have instead left the detailed exploration of the relevant areas of mathematics to the mathematician, those of philosophy to the philosopher, and those of metaphysics to anyone versed in that field of inquiry. Our efforts have been focused on examining only the elements of these disciplines that relate directly to vibration.

Because of this focus, it may seem to some that this presentation seeks to portray the universe as a single coordinating system, and therefore within the context of a total philosophical concept; but achieving comprehensiveness as a philosophy is not our intention. Rather, our aim is simply to investigate the specific theme of vibrations and how we use them. Whether or not one finds the various concepts explored in this work acceptable and meaningful, he may yet discover herein a thread worth following, like the one Ariadne left for Theseus which led him to his escape from the labyrinth.

What exactly is the nature of our Ariadne thread, and where does it lead us? As we shall find, this thread lies in the continuity of manifestation, and it leads from the simplest atom through the universe, even to a possible bridge between the physical world and God. But nowhere in these pages is there an attempt to explain God or to show what He is. God is treated as God, without pursuing the different concepts of what is meant by the term. It is true that in much of this presentation the author, like ancient and modern philosophers, seeks to trace everything back to its ultimate origin, to creation; but this is a natural and logical consequence of our search for the essence of vibration (or, as we shall see, of color), not the deliberate following of a philosophical bent.

It is, however, impossible to investigate vibration in any depth without getting into some material of a philosophical nature. Certain concepts of universal significance—such as the laws behind separation and manifestation—are dealt with. Surely the presentation on time and space is in the realm of philosophical discourse; the ideas about the "shadow world" and about form were considered by early thinkers, as were various views of the atom and the material world. But in the present treatise these classical philosophical problems are looked at from a different perspective than that of the ancient theorists. This study also includes material that might be entirely unfamiliar to some readers, such as new ideas of patience and of color.

Though the conclusions reached regarding the topics mentioned above could be argued from a philosophical angle, for our purposes this presentation approaches them from the standpoint of everyday living. As we said earlier, the intention behind this effort is not to derive a specific system of thought; it is, rather, to expose the reader to certain novel conceptions that will stimulate him to achieve a better understanding of himself. A grasp of the concept of vibration can be quite meaningful in this connection, for, as will be seen, vibration is a tool that we all use every minute of every day.

This moment-to-moment application of vibration holds the key to what is perhaps the best way to use the concepts in this study. The reader is encouraged to take each of the ideas presented here, look at it from a variety of different angles and test it in his everyday life to see how it best works for him and discover to what new insights it leads him. It is not particularly important that a person comprehend exactly what the author meant when he wrote these ideas down; the meaning that really matters is the one that each individual can discover for himself as he works with and applies this material. The fact that the author has arrived at a definition of a vibration, for example, does not mean that this is the final answer. The real answer to the question of what a vibration is must necessarily rest with the reader.

This, by the way, brings us to the starting point of our entire investigation:

What is a vibration?

Chapter One
WHAT IS A VIBRATION?

Vibrations are like the roots of a tree in the forest. The roots are there, supporting and feeding the tree, but we don't concern ourselves with them. We love the tree; do we love the roots from which it grew? "Woodman, spare that tree," we cry, but who knows an ode to the roots? Who cares about the roots, as long as they build the tree? Could we say that the tree is but a projection of the roots? Does the root have a life of its own, or does it merely serve its projection?

Do such questions evoke an insight into our perspective of a tree and its roots? As analogies, are they relevent to a concept of vibrations? Perhaps much more so than it would seem at first glance, for just as we are often caught up in our admiration of the tree without understanding or caring about its roots, in like manner we may be captivated by the results of a vibration without understanding the vibration which is the basis for that which we like.

Who needs to know more about vibrations? We know what they are. We hear them, we feel them, we use them and we make them. We like those we like and abhor those we don't like; sometimes we don't like those we make, but who cares? What could be wrong with concentrating on just our reactions to the vibrations that come to us and not bothering to look at the vibrations themselves? Surely he who keeps a flower growing knows that he waters the roots and not the flower. Does understanding the vibration itself really matter? If such an understanding brings us closer to grasping the true nature of reality, then it does matter.

It has long been known that we hear by way of vibrations. After Newton, light came to be recognized as vibration, and at the

1

present time almost everyone realizes that the stimulus to which we react is indeed vibration. We all have sensed some vibrations we like and some we do not like. We tend to take vibration for granted and think of it as merely a back-and-forth movement of some kind. Most people believe they know what a vibration is, yet they would have difficulty in arriving at a satisfactory definition of one. According to general opinion, a good definition of vibration could be found in most dictionaries; for example:

"Vibration: (1) act of vibrating; oscillation; (2) state of vibrating; tremulous effect. (3) Physics: (a) the oscillating, reciprocating or other periodic motion of a rigid or elastic body forced from a position or state of equilibrium; (b) the analogous motion of the particles of a mass of air, etc., whose state of equilibrium has been disturbed, as in transmitting sound, etc.; (c) the vibratory motion of a string or other sonorous body, producing musical sound; (4) a single vibrating motion; an oscillation; a quiver or tremor."

In relation to these definitions, we know that light is vibration, as is sound. It is known that light is sensed by us because its various rates of vibration fall within a certain range. Outside this range are other types of vibration: infrared, ultraviolet, radio waves, X-rays, etc. Sound, of course, we liken to waves, whereas light we understand to be either waves or particles, for in the laboratory it sometimes acts as waves and sometimes as particles. While this phenomenon may be interesting, our concern is with vibration, not with the exact nature of light.

The words in the above definition seem not to mean too much, seem to lead us around and around without telling us much about what a vibration really is. Could it be that the definition makers, like most of us, are just taking vibration as a matter of fact without trying to look at it more deeply? A question that we might find intriguing is: If we look hard enough, can we expect to find a really meaningful understanding of vibration? If we dare to take this challenge, we could be surprised, especially if we are willing to follow the meaning of words as we might follow roots in the forest.

Vibrations and the Senses

Let us start with something of which we are aware—sound. We get a concept relative to sound from watching ripples on water.

From a stone dropped into a pond the ripples radiate outward equally in all directions. We know that the sound of our voices radiates from us in much the same manner. Air is the medium carrying this vibration. In the first instance the stone pushes against the water and causes the ripple, whereas in the second the voice box pushes against air and we hear the sound. We know that sound travels much better through water than through air. Does the medium carrying a vibration have anything to do with the vibration itself? See if you can answer this question.

Now we have opened a whole field of inquiry about vibration; we are examining the idea that vibration moves through, or by way of, a medium. This concept gives rise to two questions: Does vibration need a medium through which to move? And, if so, is the vibration affected by the medium? Though the answers may seem obvious, and perhaps trite, they are quite meaningful when we look a little deeper. Of course, considering these two questions forces us to face yet another, the one that led to this study. That question is: Does vibration have an essence *other* than that which the dictionary definitions imply? These definitions relate more to results, to how vibrations of certain kinds are made, than to vibration *per se*. Since the definitions mention light and sound, they open for us the possibility of looking at all five of our senses and how they use vibration. This, in turn, leads us to the question of how we form meaningful vibrations, as in speech. Each of these fields of inquiry is worth considering along with the question of the essence of vibration itself. Certainly the fact that in speech we put meaning into a vibration is intriguing, especially as it relates to the postulated essence of vibration.

Let us now consider our five senses and see if we can learn something that may be useful in our search.

We say that we hear with our ears. If one thinks about this for a moment, it is readily seen that the statement is not true. The ear is actually a mechanical device which transforms the vibration of sound into electrical impulses that travel along nerves leading to the brain, which in turn interprets these impulses into the experience of words, music or whatnot. It may well be said that we do not hear anything; rather, we use our ears as mechanical devices to transform vibrations that are carried through the medium of air into electrical impulses, which in turn are interpreted by the brain.

Similarly, we say that we see with our eyes. But like the ears, the eyes are used as mechanical devices for the brain to interpret certain vibrations reaching them. A difference, though, is that seemingly it is not necessary for the vibrations received by the eye to be carried by a medium of any nature whatsoever, for light travels through a vacuum better than through air or water. While sound travels through air and water but not through a vacuum, light travels best through a vacuum, less well through air, poorly through water, and not at all through opaque solids. The instance of light would suggest that the medium is not important, but this will be examined again in a different context, in which the importance of the medium is demonstrated.

So much for sight and hearing, but what about the other three senses—smell, taste and touch. Do we have mechanical devices here also, as the eyes and ears, which help us interpret vibration?

In the case of smell the olfactory nerves certainly transmit vibration to the brain in a fashion similar to that of vision and audition; but in this instance the vibration sensed must be carried by a gaseous medium, such as air, and no sense of smell can be experienced if this medium is absent. Within a vacuum one could not use the sense of smell to learn the qualities of pepper. The taste buds on the tongue work quite similarly to the olfactory nerves. Smell and taste are primarily distinguished from each other not by the way in which they function, but by the medium that carries the vibration which is to be interpreted. Thus, the sense of smell extracts the vibrations from a gas, while taste extracts the vibrations from solids and liquids. The gustatory and olfactory nerves both transmit to the brain certain electrical impulses by which we learn certain qualities of solids and gases, just as we do through the optic and auditory nerves.

Though the sense of touch is similar to sight in that we use it to discern the forms of objects, the vibrations transmitted through this sense give us some information about form that is not otherwise obtainable. Thus touch and sight tend to substantiate each other, but in a way that is tentative, not certain. This is illustrated in the story of the five blind men, each of whom tried to deduce the form of an elephant by feeling a different part of its body. Our sense of touch also relates to speech, for with our voice box we push against air until, through trial and error, we identify how it feels to make various sounds; eventually we learn to control this activity so that we can produce different words and come to speak clearly. In a sense we have come full circle back to the stone pushing against water to make waves.

What does all this have to do with vibration? It indicates that before we can consider the question of what a vibration is we must learn more about our sensing abilities. If we seek to follow the admonition "know thyself," it is important that we first investigate our sensing processes.

From the above concepts and their implications we can derive the following statements relevant to our study of vibration:

1. Through our five senses we learn or comprehend certain characteristics of things, mostly by way of a medium.

2. These characteristics may or may not be directly related to the essences of the things we perceive.

3. While we may or may not knowingly receive vibrations directly from all things perceived by our senses, the sense mechanisms set up vibrations (electrical impulses) within our nervous system which we first sense and then go on to interpret in the light of that previously learned or being learned at present. The learning process will be dealt with later.

4. We generally do not know much about vibrations except that they are like the waves made by a stone dropped in water.

5. Though most people are aware of vibrations as related to sound, touch and sight, they have not thought too much about the way in which vibration is related to taste and smell. However, anyone who considers the question seriously will readily realize that all the senses actually operate by way of vibration.

6. While we are aware in a general way that we use vibrations and react to them according to our likes and dislikes, we usually view our reactions as being due more to the circumstances in which we find ourselves than to the vibrations that in reality are the cause of our positive or negative feelings. But are not those circumstances only shadows of a deeper reality?

7. Vibrations act as stimuli to the five sensory receptors. But does the vibration cause any of its own essence to be transmitted to the brain along with the electrical impulse it arouses? Or are we stimulated only to remember what we already know or to learn something new by analyzing concepts stored in our memory? In other words, is a vibration *merely* a stimulus? If so, perhaps we need not bother with further investigation of what a vibration may be.

Vibration and Color

Before trying to answer this question, we should review our dictionary definition of vibration and look up a related word or two. Since we all are aware that sound is vibration, let us consider how the dictionary defines *music:* "An art of sound in time which expresses ideas and emotions in significant forms through the elements of rhythm, melody, harmony, and color." But are not color and vibration one and the same? Oh no, one says, for color is merely one segment of the vibratory scale which stimulates the optic nerves of the eye and which we know as light, there being seven spectromatic colors seen in this range. But others say that not only are they aware of colors through sight, they actually experience music as colors. Consider the following:

Dr. Peter F. Ostwald, of the University of California Department of Psychiatry, San Francisco, tells of a young woman who always sees various colors when she hears different words or sounds. This hearing of words and seeing colors simultaneously is called synesthesia. Dr. Ostwald has estimated that 14 percent of the male population and 31 percent of the female experience some form of this phenomenon.

Kristian Holt-Hansen, a Danish psychologist, has conducted experiments related to synesthesia, wherein he demonstrates that sensations in one sensory modality carry with them impressions in another sensory modality ("An Experiment in Sound," *Parapsychology Review*, November-December, 1968). His theory is that there is a point of crossover where the different senses join to create a single experience.

Here a question is in order. Since a certain percentage of people experience this synesthesia between color and sound, is it possible that all people actually experience this crossover but just are not aware of doing so? Is it possible that we get into the habit of paying so much attention to that seemingly sensed that we become unaware of how we are sensing it? Are we content to keep taking our senses for granted, or will we recognize how important these questions are if we are to know ourselves?

Since this sensing crossover of synesthesia is pretty well established as a scientific fact, at least for some people, and since all the sense impressions seem to cross over to color and not vice versa, we should ask the question *why.* Why do we not have a color crossover to taste or words? If the crossover is always into color, surely there must be an explanation which would help us to know more about ourselves and how the body—perhaps even the soul—functions.

Edgar Cayce had this to say:

> . . . as we find in the physical body that sight, hearing, taste, speech, are but an alteration of vibration attuned to those portions in the consciousness of the physical body, becoming aware *of* things, *of* vibration, reaching same from within or from without.   281-4

While the above questions must be answered, it may be more appropriate for us to call attention to some of the items the questions imply rather than discussing the answers themselves, for the implications may disclose the answers to some of our previous questions.

Since all things perceived through the five senses are quite possibly experienced as color, it appears that we have here a common denominator to everything we perceive; but perhaps this common denominator is not real in itself, but merely a shadow of that intended to be sensed. Thus it would be color that brings us the idea and the purpose behind anything we perceive.[1] Could this be possible? Must we stretch our imaginations in yet another direction before going on with our study of vibrations? This concept might give us a clue to understanding the shadow world of which Plato spoke—a cave in which we perceive only shadows but interpret these shadows as being real, until we experience a greater reality. Perhaps the meaning of this cave analogy is one of the items that will be clarified by a study of vibration.

Another matter which should be noted is that somehow all things must have an essence not related to their sensory form, texture or appearance. The mind must initially need to experience this essence as color; if this were not true, why would color be the common factor in all our sensing? A related question is, is that which is experienced through the senses present simply to fill a need of the mind that does the sensing? If not, why is anything sensed? If there is such a need, why does it exist? These questions too will become more meaningful as we continue this study.

---

[1]This concept will be considered extensively later on and will become more clear as we continue this study.

If the foregoing statements about our sensing process are true—that we actually are initially aware only of those vibrations we may come to know as color, and that there may be a need to comprehend anything that is perceived—then there must of necessity be an essence behind or in color; thus color, too, is only a shadow. In other words, we need to seek an answer to the question of what color—or, perhaps, the reality that casts its shadow as color—is. These questions are central to the whole development of this study. This entire work is based upon the thesis that behind the experience of our five senses there is the common denominator of color, and color is but a shadow of a deeper reality.

Subliminal Reception

Color is not all we should look at, however, for there are other factors that must be considered. In order to get an idea of how we might do this, let us look at one of the first nonphysical readings Edgar Cayce gave.

Q-41. Give the best method of helping the human family increase in knowledge of the subconscious soul or spirit world.

A-41. The knowledge of the subconscious of an entity, or an individual, in or of the human family, is as of one integral force, or element, or self in the creation of the human family, and until the entity, or individual, as individuals, make this known to groups, classes, countries, nations, *the greater study of self,* that force will only be magnified. That of the spirit is the spark, or portion of the Divine that is in every entity, whether complete or of the evolution to that completeness.

The study from the human standpoint, of subconscious, *subliminal,* psychic, soul forces, is and should be the great study for the human family, for through self man will understand its *Maker* when it understands its relation to its *Maker,* and it will only understand that through itself, and that understanding is the knowledge as is given here in this state. [Author's italics]   3744-4

One may readily note the reference to the "subliminal," which calls to mind Dr. Ostwald's experiments on synesthesia, as well as the postulate that all people actually experience this, though most do so subliminally. It will be seen that in our search for a meaning and the uses of vibration we will be dealing largely with this concept, synesthesia, and how it relates to all five of the senses. As we move into the ramifications of our study, it will be well to keep the above quotation in mind, for our study involves the *self*.

"Subliminal" is the key word that we need to notice in this quotation because what is perceived by us subliminally can sometimes be the controlling factor in our reactions. It is well known that isolated picture frames bearing the suggestion to "eat popcorn," when placed within a movie, stir the audience to rush to the popcorn stand after the film. In fact, the power of this method of suggestion is so devastating that federal law now forbids its use. The point to be gained here is that much of what we respond to in another is sensed subliminally; this is the case of anything perceived.

That the action of subliminal perception is most important to us will be noted later, especially as we consider just how we perceive anything. This study is predicated on the proposition that if we can know more about the workings of the subconscious, subliminal and unconscious minds, we perhaps can gain some understanding not only of ourselves, but also of vibrations and how we use them.

Summary

It might be well now to summarize our findings so far, so that we can arrive at a cohesive concept of the direction our investigation of vibrations will take. This study may well prove difficult to follow, especially because of the seeming diversions, such as those into the five senses and the sensing process. Yet these too are involved even in a beginning study of vibration; they are among the roots we must attempt to trace if we are to come to know better the tree that grows from them. If we find that the tree is really a projection of the roots, then the roots serve their own projection.

We may find this analogy to be instructive regarding the nature of man as we know him, for he may in actuality be a projection of spirit which has taken on materiality. Thus our present perception of man may, as in Plato's analogy of the cave, be a perception of a shadow, behind which lies a greater reality.

The main points considered in this chapter, though not necessarily in the order in which they have been introduced, are:

1. Though generally we all admit that we are involved with vibrations, we are far more involved with them than may at first seem obvious.

2. In order to understand something about vibrations, we need to look at how we use them.

3. Our five senses bring us differing qualities of vibrations and are necessary for comprehending their essences, which in turn are as varied as our knowledge and potentials of understanding.

4. The five senses bring to us an understanding of vibrations and their essences by way of color, which is a *shadow* of the essences. Thus we have postulated that all things are sensed by us as color, regardless of the source of the stimulus.

Chapter Two
THE ATOMIC WORLD

We started with a statement likening vibrations to the roots of trees; they are there, whether we are aware of them or not. If we can accept the idea that the roots really serve the trees that are their projections, we may find that this analogy is not at all far fetched. Our exploration into the nature of vibrations and how we use them has led us through a maze that could easily boggle the imagination; yet who can follow the statements and questions to which these wanderings have led us without feeling that somehow there must be some answer yet to be perceived? The study of vibration is really as all-encompassing as a study of the Bible, or perhaps—because of its ramifications—more so. This presentation is intended to be a challenge as well as a stimulus to a deeper and more comprehensive study that, it is hoped, may be made by others with more technical training.

Color and the Work of Newton and Goethe

Since we may say that we translate all impressions gained through the five senses into color, we need to consider *why*. A relevant question is, what is color? As can be seen from the following comments from the Edgar Cayce readings, color is simply vibration.

For as has been given, color is but vibration. Vibration is movement. Movement is activity of a positive and negative force.
281-29

Q-1. . . . Do the colors vary for each [endocrine] center with different individuals, or may definite colors be associated with each center?

A-1. Both. For ... as is known, vibration is the essence or the basis of color.   **281-30**

These two excerpts contain some pertinent points relative to a study of vibration. The first quote not only makes the point that "color is but vibration," but also states that *"movement is activity of a . . . force."* (Author's italics) The second reading, relating colors to the endocrine system, affirms that "vibration is the *essence* or the *basis* of color." (Author's italics) Also, there is an intimation that the endocrine system has something to do with our sensing of the colors. While these two readings indicate that we may be sensing *forces* by way of color, they also point to our need to know more about color itself before we can examine this idea in greater detail.

It is well known that there are three primary colors in the pigments—red, yellow and blue. But in light, of the seven colors of the spectrum, four are primary—red, yellow, blue and violet. A question that apparently has not evoked too much interest among scientists may well be asked: Why this difference? The fact, for example, that mixing yellow and blue pigments makes green is beside the point here, for this study is concerned not with colors *per se,* but with vibrations.[2] Those wishing to pursue this matter might find pertinent corollary study in the divergent opinions expressed by Goethe and Newton about color and its significance.

For our purposes, however, a brief overview of the work of these two men will suffice. Newton's theories have led to spectroscopy (in which chemicals can be identified on the basis of mathematical calculations involving the colors they emit) and have allowed the study of optics to develop to the point where it can be called an exact science. On the other hand, those of Goethe have been relegated primarily to the esoterics of artists and poets because they seem to deal more with appreciation of the intrinsic value of each color—what the color means. It can be said that the major difference between the ideas of the two theorists involves the level at which each conducted his analysis—that is, the objective level at which Newton worked versus the subjective one

---

[2] It might be helpful to point out that while most people feel that the mixture of blue and yellow makes green, this effect is due only to impurities in the *pigments* that are being used. In working with *light,* however, it is found that combining spectral blue with spectral yellow yields a gray bordering on white. This effect was elucidated by Helmholtz in the mid-19th century.

that was Goethe's main concern—rather than conflicting views of reality itself. Yet both men worked primarily with the colors of light and not those of the pigments, and, so far as is known, neither asked the question of why there are four primary colors in light and only three in the pigments. At first glance, this study of vibrations may seem more appreciative of Goethe's theories than of Newton's, yet the two are equally important if the study is to lead to the understanding hoped for.

Goethe spoke of the "appreciation" of life sensed through colors. Could this somehow be equated with the "positive and negative force" mentioned earlier in reading 281-29? Was he "seeing through a glass darkly" to a reality felt and not understood?

Goethe is also credited with the idea of a color circle wherein three pairs of complementary, or "demanded," colors lie opposite each other. He claimed that the cause of this demand is physiological; yet, if we accept his view that each color has a meaning, the need could well be psychological also, for with the perceptions of one concept we "need" to perceive the opposite. Thus there would seem to be a "demand" that we also see the opposite of anything being seen. In other words, with every perception there is portrayed, to our subconscious, the law of opposites. How could the law of balance work if we did not see both sides of everything we perceive? The significance of Goethe's color circle cannot be overlooked in any investigation of vibration, especially this one, as will be seen when we get to the study of the glandular activities and of time, space and patience. The harmonies or "demanded" activities could well be the subject of a whole separate treatise.[3]

At this point, the importance of mathematics to an understanding of vibration should be stressed. If we follow the

---

[3]The importance of "demanded" colors will grow more evident later on in this study, once we have identified the concept to which each color corresponds. Placing these concepts in the appropriate areas of Goethe's color circle, we find that time (orange) demands we know purpose (blue), growth (?) (green) demands we know relationships (indigo), and an idea (yellow) demands we know patience (violet). Though at this point the derivation of these correspondences is no doubt unclear to the reader, they should be carefully followed throughout the subsequent portions of our study; their impact will become clearer as we progress. The color meanings are noted here in order to point to the law of opposites as being at all times portrayed to us (though subconsciously perceived), whereas we usually think of this law as only being an intellectual process by which we will eventually come to place all things in their proper perspective.

ramifications of Newton's work related to optics and the mathematics of color, whereby the colors emitted by the various elements can be predicted with certainty (some elements that were missing from the periodic table were predicted on the basis of the mathematics of color), we will become aware that math is involved not only in an understanding of color but also in the atomic structure of the elements. Edgar Cayce said that music and mathematics were the building blocks of the universe; but we have now seen that music is color, and color is vibration. So what is vibration but light? Let us now consider vibration as light.

What is light? While the first definition given of light is usually one that pertains to physics, an equally acceptable one is that inferred in the expression "to throw light on a subject," meaning to give help toward a better understanding of that subject. The phrase "I see" is commonly used to mean "I comprehend" or "I understand." It might seem that this definition and the physical one are unrelated, but may there not be a deeper relationship between the realities of the physics of light and the experience of "seeing" as "understanding"? When we consider that we comprehend all vibration as color, it should certainly be easy for us to conceive that in reality the only light there is is that of understanding. *We* who comprehend are—so to speak—merely sitting back in darkness and being aware of vibrations that reach us through our senses. Our interpretation of these vibrations leads us to believe that we *see*. This *seeing* we relate to vibrations obtained through all the senses, not just sight. Understanding, then, is a more all-encompassing definition for light than that supplied by physics; this is why we say that this study follows Goethe's approach rather than Newton's. The definition of light as understanding, however, poses another question: Just what is understanding?

If we reflect upon these considerations, we may begin to comprehend that light or color comprehension is in actuality a sensing of *forces* that move in the vibrations we become aware of through our senses. Could sensing, then, involve not only a movement of the vibrations sensed, but also a movement within consciousness from nonawareness to awareness?

The Law of Separation and the Law of Oneness
Another aspect of vibration worth looking into involves its

14

"positive and negative force," as mentioned in reading 281-29. What is meant here by "positive" and "negative"? All too often we think of vibrations as being good or bad according to whether we like them or don't like them; and we have a tendency to classify all vibrations which we do not like as being bad, or negative, and those that we do like as being good, or positive. In other words, we generally equate "positive" with "good" and "negative" with "bad"; but this relates more to our likes and dislikes than to the actual positive or negative aspect of the force. As used in this reading, that "movement [which] is activity of a positive and negative force" is no doubt related to "the force of attraction and the force that repelled" (262-52) that Edgar Cayce tells us was operative in the initial creation. Could it be, then, that the positive or negative aspects of *movement* are determined not by our likes and dislikes, but by the *kind* of movement that is taking place? A buzz saw could be destructive to a finger, but creative when used properly for its purposes. If we were to continue focusing on just our likes and dislikes, we would have a hard time deciding whether this movement should be characterized as positive or as negative.

How should one picture a positive vibration? A negative one? How would one picture a positive movement as opposite to a negative one? If you were asked to draw a line, what would it look like? Would it be a straight line? Then how long, and why would it be straight? Would you draw a crooked line, a jagged one, or a curved one? If so, how crooked, or jagged, or curved? And in what direction would you draw it—from left to right, or right to left? From top to bottom, or bottom to top? And with what would you draw it? These questions may seem trite, but considering them can prove most pertinent to an understanding of what kind of movement is meant in this reading, for Edgar Cayce said "movement," which seems to mean movement *per se;* yet it is movement that depends upon an *activity.* In another reading we find:

In the beginning there was the force of attraction and the force that repelled.   **262-52**

Not only does this quotation point up the positive and negative aspects of vibration, as well as the law "like attracts like," but it implies one of the most fundamental of laws relative to man. In fact, man would not exist but for this law, which has its foundation in the original creation of souls before the creation of the world. This is the Law of Separation, which relates to the "negative force" and "the force that repelled"; it has so much to do with understanding vibrations—and with knowing anything at all—that it cannot be overlooked.

In fact, this law is evident as a *need*, in Genesis 1:4: "And God saw the light, that it was good; and God *divided* the light from the darkness," for God had created heaven and earth, and the "earth was without form, and void; and darkness was upon the face of the deep." (Gen. 1:2) In the initial creation, this Law of Separation was necessary to bring order out of chaos.

Now, as to why this law needs to be mentioned here, it is simply that, in order to begin our study of vibrations, we must "separate" the roots in the forest. Since vibrations are positive or negative according to their activity, we must find a common denominator between them, for Edgar Cayce has said that "all force is one force" and "all life is one life"—there are just different manifestations of it. Let us now examine this principle of oneness; we will return later in this study to a consideration of the Law of Separation.

If Edgar Cayce is right, all vibration is one vibration, for he says,

All force is vibration, as all comes from one central vibration... [just] taking different form.   900-422

Maybe we cannot find the smallest vibration or root, but can we find the simplest one? Or could we possibly find a *universal* vibration which takes different forms? Remember, the earth was without form and void until light was created and separated from darkness and the waters under the firmament were divided from the waters above the firmament. Could it be that what makes one vibration *seem* different from another has something to do with the medium through which we sense it? Could it be that to a universal vibration there is added that substance needed to form the various manifestations? Is there a basis for such an assumption in the Cayce readings?

That various forces are active upon and through the earth and that these activities are thus perceived by our senses are pointed to in the following:

> ... the activities of *other influences* in those forces or sources of activity *condensed in form to be called matter* ... [Author's italics]
> 262-55

Then *matter* is but the *form* of *forces*, and forms are in fact media that express the influence necessary for our comprehension of the forces themselves, for those "conditions that exist in the material plane are but shadows of the truths in the mental and spiritual plane." (262-55)

> ... for matter is an expression of spirit in motion to such a degree as to give the expressions in materiality.
> ... just as each atom is made up of urges according to the movement of and with what? That which in its final analysis is the mind of that Creative Energy which has called into being the mind that is a portion of self... That *is* as from the beginning, that *each thought of the Creator bore within itself its* OWN *fruit as from the beginning.* [Author's italics]
> 262-78

Within these quotations may be found the *essence* of the vibrations that compose the manifest *material* world. (We will come to the nonmaterial, yet manifest, world later.) Let us follow God's steps in creation and try to get an analogy of the *materially* manifesting vibration.

In the beginning, God *created*—thus there was *movement*, an *expression of spirit*, but the expressions were not *formed;* yet the movement, or creation, contained every thought of the Creator as a potential of expression. Here is vibration at its highest state of expression—one movement expressing the ALL, yet *void* of expressing *any one thing* because there was no *separation* of thoughts or understandings, let alone of manifestations. Here is that *Being/non-Being*, the All in All, that unexpressible oneness men have striven to find—and yet can never find, for man conceives only by, and under the grace of, the Law of Separation. This law he can never transcend, for his destiny is eventually to be one with, equal to yet *separate* from, the Creator.

Consider this passage, from 262-78 above: "... the mind of that Creative Energy which has called into being the mind that is a

17

portion of self." Here is expressed the Father-Son relationship in *every* thing there is! (And—like attracts like! It is almost as if we *must* be attracted to our Creator; but that is yet another part of our study that will be considered later.)

Now we, who can conceive an idea *only* under this Law of Separation, must try to divide this *oneness*—this original movement—into separated parts so that we can begin to understand ourselves. By the *grace of God* we are given the tools with which we may be able to do this. Actually, it is through this very law—*manifested* as time, space and patience—that we are able to conceive of our oneness with our Maker, would we but awaken to our potential of understanding. But this, too, will be dealt with later in our study, for consider the *when* factors mentioned in the following statements by Edgar Cayce:

The following of those sources, forces, activities that are in accord with the creative force or first cause—its laws, then—is to be one with the source, or equal with yet separate from that first cause. When, then, may man—as an element, an entity, a *separate* being manifested in material life and form—be aware or conscious of the moving of that first cause within his own environ? Or, taking man in his present position or consciousness, how or *when* may he be aware of that first cause moving within his realm of consciousness?

In the beginning there was the force of attraction and the force that repelled. Hence, in man's consciousness he becomes aware of what is known as the atomic or cellular form of movement about which there becomes nebulous activity. And this is the lowest form...that's in active forces in his experience. Yet this very movement that *separates the forces* in atomic influence IS the first cause, or the manifestation of that called God in the material plane! [Author's italics]   262-52

When? When we *follow* those laws! In the following excerpt the above concepts are expressed in another way:

In analyzing self, the entity finds itself body, mind and soul, that answers in the three-dimensional plane to the Godhead—Father, Son, Holy Spirit. God moved, the spirit came into activity. In moving it brought light, and then chaos. In this light came creation of that which in the earth came to be matter; in the spheres about the earth, space and time; and in patience it has evolved through those activities until there are the heavens and all the constellations, the stars, the universe as it is known—or sought to be known by individual soul-entities in the material plane.

3508-1

Again we are called upon to analyze ourselves within the framework of all that man comprehends about the total creation—the manifested creation, that is.

In this reading it seems evident that space and time were necessary as corollary activities, or principles, and later we will discuss these concepts or dimensions more specifically as they relate to the creation of matter. It is in the dimensions of time and space that we become aware of the separate manifested forms of thought. For the manifested world seems to express the separate potentials of that Mind that created the ALL in the first place, for *all* was in that Mind in the beginning.

In 262-52 we see that man "becomes aware of what is known as the atomic or cellular form of movement . . ." At this point, in order to know what the atoms—in their essences—manifest, we need to look at another aspect of the *form of movement* as comprehended by man. The readings again supply some answers that point our way, for remember, the earth was without *form!* The light (understanding or, as in John 1:1, the Word, the Logos) brought the *form* of matter; thus, the material building blocks of the manifested universe are in essence but *formed separated* expressions of that Mind that moved in the first place for "each thought of the Creator bore within itself its *own* fruit as from the beginning." (262-78)

Through the *essences* of the forms, not the forms themselves, we may come to know *what* is being expressed by them as we in patience evolve "through those activities" until we may become that one-with-the-whole we are inherently seeking to be. Before investigating why we should pay attention to the essence and not the form, let us consider another question this statement gives rise to: How do we even know what we are seeking? By becoming aware of ourselves. How do we become aware? Or why should we, even if we were capable of doing so? This seems very much like our original question of why we should study vibrations. Edgar Cayce gave one response which seems to answer both questions— though his reply is either trite or profound, according to how each of us reacts to it.

As to self's being awakened, or aware of, that depends upon what is being referred to. As to the *abilities* of self to become conscious of, or aware of, all are endowed with that, will they but be awakened or aroused to the necessity of becoming aware of.   262-23

The Law of Reflection

What can we become aware of about atomic forces that will help us in our study of vibration? The point made above—that we must look to the essence of these forces rather than their forms—is indicated in the following quotations; and yet, by the form we may come to know more of the essence. These readings are quoted for a single purpose—to show that what we see in a *thing* is not *really* what is being seen.

... all one sees manifest in a material world is but a *reflection* or a shadow of the real or the spiritual life ...
That made manifest in a third-dimensional plane, or materialization, is a shadow or *reflection* of that from which it has its emanation! [Author's italics]   262-23

Though these readings were quoted for just one purpose, they illustrate the fact that Cayce rarely made an explanatory statement that bore information relating only to the idea being explained. Within these two readings there is implied another concept—the Law of Reflection—which is absolutely necessary to gaining an understanding of the atom and its essences. This is one of the greatest truths, or laws, relative to the universe and our understanding of it; it is just as basic to our process of comprehension, and just as obvious, as the Law of Separation, or time and space. It is so common and we use it so much, by just taking it for granted, that for the most part man has never considered it to be a law at all. But the main point is that the operation of the Law of Reflection is necessary before we can even be aware of time and space.

When we study the concept of reflection and entertain the notion that it does exist as a law of nature, we may realize that Plato's story of the shadows in the cave is more meaningful than we have heretofore envisioned. For, if all things in the material plane are mere *shadows*, then Plato was really right; he was not, as we may have thought, merely making a point. We *are* still living with those shadows in the cave and *thinking* we see the real!

Earlier in our discussion we emphasized the importance of the medium for vibrations. Let us now see how this relates to the Law of Reflection. Light falls on an object and the object becomes a *medium* for reflecting the light to us. The reflected light carries qualities related to the object that were not present in the original light. Thus, the vibration sensed by us is a modified vibration carrying information about the object not otherwise obtainable by us. It is by the light reflected from the object that we perceive its form and other qualities; through this process we obtain knowledge that can be utilized if we should encounter the object in other circumstances.

If an object did not reflect light in some fashion or cast its shadow toward us as a silhouette, we could not see it. Also, if we could not *reflect upon* that object when it is seen, we could not remember having previously seen it. Thus it is by internal *reflection* that we remember anything at all. When we see an object that we have never before noticed or known anything about, we reflect upon it, comparing it with other objects, ones that we know (remember). This internal process is exactly the same as the external one, for we reflect upon the mental image of that externally reflected image—and both are comprehended by way of vibration. As can be seen, reflection is so much a part and parcel of our learning process that if we did not use it we would always be seeing everything anew, and so we would never learn anything. Thus we use the Law of Reflection to comprehend that reflected by the manifested world.

Through this process of internal and external reflection we come to know that all material things reflect light in some way. What else can we say about material objects in general? We know that they are all composed of atoms, and science has proved that each atom is made up of particles that move in such a manner as to produce seemingly stable elements which comprise what is called—in totality—the manifested universe. Let us now consider the single atom.

The Atom

As you may remember, the ancient Greeks used the word *atom* to refer to the smallest particle of matter. When modern science determined that the natural elements were made of (supposedly) permanent particles, those particles were called atoms, and men thought they had discovered the atoms the old Greeks had talked about. But since each single atom, as we use the word today, is composed of particles of various and sundry natures—all in motion, yet somehow held together to form the various natural chemical elements—it is evident that these atoms are not the smallest particles. We can now see that the Greeks were talking about the *particles* of what we call atoms rather than the atoms themselves, as was once contended.

All these particles, though in constant movement, are held together in geometric configurations in such a way that they are the building blocks of the manifested universe. This, too, the Greeks recognized; but even during their time it seemed to them that some qualities, such as those experienced as taste, hardness, and acidity, could not be expressed geometrically. While it would be nice to include here a summary of the centuries-old dialogues about this issue, the point being made here is that, with the use of the Law of Reflection, all the obstacles to understanding the phenomena of geometric forms as related to *all* material qualities may be overcome; in this way we may approach a concept of the oneness of all things. But this concept may not be comprehended unless we realize that the Law of Separation and the Law of Reflection work equally and in conjunction with the geometric patterns. In fact, it might be argued that without these two laws, geometry could not be known at all.

Furthermore, regarding the ramifications of geometry, one might agree with Plato, who argued that the physical properties of matter are built on geometrical components, which in turn are simple triangles (the attendant square being a derivative thereof). Out of such a study one might gain concepts more relevant to creation than would at first be suspected. Why? Because, by way of reflection, the geometry of the triangle (and thus of all manifestation) is the foundation of the three basic colors in the pigments. And, since these colors are shadows of the real, through understanding this aspect of the Law of Reflection we can ascertain the composition of the expression of the Trinity inherent in the whole atomic gamut of manifestation.[4] It is thus that man gains a concept of the oneness of all things which lies in the essence of the ALL as it is present throughout materiality. How and why he does this is the reason for this study of vibration.

[4]For a corollary study, see Schopenhauer's *The World as Idea.*

It may seem that so far in our study we have wandered into many fields not necessarily related to vibration. But in fact they constitute a necessary corollary study in our attempt to comprehend the essences involved, and without this basic comprehension we cannot reach a meaningful understanding of vibration. Part and parcel of this presentation is the contention that the words used in defining a vibration are so simple that, unless we grasp the implications of the laws they express, they are liable to seem trivial. The simplicity of these words can cause us to underestimate their importance, leading us to ask, "So what?" But this very feeling of "So what," when it involves a serious inquiry, has been the basis of all scientific and theological discussion throughout the ages. The hope is that it ever remains a spur to man to search for a meaning to himself and his being.

Spiritual Principles as Expressed in the Geometry of the Atom

It is interesting that sometimes from old thoughts there comes a new awareness. Such an awareness might come to one who has noted Plato's contention that all atomic forms, though geometric, are in essence composed of triangles and has related this to the fact that there are only three basic colors in the pigments. That there is more than ample reason for considering such a connection—in fact, that the very essence of a vibration is involved—will become more evident as we move along. This relationship, though, points to the necessity of our effort to study some of the properties of the atomic world before we try to understand vibration.

We are reminded again of Edgar Cayce's statements that "matter is an expression of spirit in motion" (262-78) and man "becomes aware of what is known as the atomic...movement..." (262-52) These two quotations have been chosen because they are most pointed in their statements about what *form* an expression might take. It seems that the material world, then, takes geometric forms for the purpose of expressing those "shadows of the *truths* in the mental and spiritual plane" [Author's italics] (266-55) by way of the movement within the form; and this "in its final analysis is the *mind*..." [Author's italics] (262-78)

Let us now look at some of the forms to see if we can identify the truths they are shadows of; perhaps a few illustrations will be sufficient to indicate the principles involved. Plato's simple triangle may be considered the basis of all manifested things, and the simplest triangle is the equilateral. Isn't it most evident that this form could be a shadow of the Trinity—Father, Son and Holy Spirit—showing by the three points at its corners their equality (reflected in its three equal sides), and at the same time being an expression, in materiality, of the one force that is (according to Plato) the basis for any and all materiality? Before we move on to other forms, let us consider for a moment the scalene triangle, wherein the three sides are unequal; but would anyone question that the points at its corners are yet equal? Is the difference between the two triangles, then, only in the *form?* If so, then the form of the scalene triangle, while still an expression of the Trinity, carries yet another idea to man—that of the *variableness* of the Trinity's expression in and through the material world. For "matter is an expression of *spirit in motion* ... as to give the *expressions* in materiality," [Author's italics] (262-78) and "the manifestation of that called God in the material plane!" (262-52)

Of course, much more could be said about the triangle and its symbology, but for our study here we would look at one other question raised by the foregoing and then move on to another form. That question is: Can we really conceive that the triangle *manifested* in the atomic world is in reality a manifestation of God? This statement was made by Edgar Cayce, but does the fact that he made it prove it to be true? One might intellectually accept such an idea, but it seems that Cayce himself (that is, in the readings) did not expect the statement to be much more than a guide, for he insisted that only by experiencing the Christ way of living might we come to know our oneness with our Creator. But this does not negate the importance of our looking behind material forms in an attempt to discern the spiritual truths they express, for by doing so we may get a glimmer of the meaning of our separation from our Maker and an indication of our way back to Him. The opportunity we have of comprehending by way of vibrations these myriad expressions shows forth the love of the Father for the prodigal son.[5]

Let us now consider another form, one that seems logically and necessarily to follow from the triangle: the square. Here we find

---

[5]That no man can *see* God is something else to think about, for no man can see an atom, let alone its particles or vibrations. Also, no one can *see* light— we see only the object from which light is reflected or the source of light.

that the Law of Cause and Effect is exemplified in the "sum of the squares," as is the truth that can be termed at this point the Law of Sequences and Equality, which states that the result is equal to the cause (as expressed, for example, in $E=mc^2$). Remember, here we are talking only about the manifested *truths* found in forms of atomic structures. The square alone manifests truths not necessarily flowing from the triangle, and yet within the square is found all the forms of the triangle. Here seems to be a basis for an understanding of the statement that "each thought of the Creator bore within itself its *own* fruit as from the beginning." (262-78) The square bears within itself all the potentials of the triangle from which it springs. Could this be yet another manifested truth? The square, of course, exemplifies many more truths, such as the "closed" thought, the end and equality. These are too numerous for us to go into their details here, for our purpose is not to explain what in particular the various forms manifest; rather, it is to point out that the forms present to us truths, thoughts or perhaps laws.

The circle, of course, is the form thought of as the most universal symbol, showing both the wholeness of creation and the sun, which in turn symbolizes the Deity. It is an appropriate representation of the totality of nature's manifestations; it can be taken as the shadow of the complete process of evolution, in which all things pass through materiality and come full circle back to their origin (returning to the Father). Thus the circle could well be seen as the embodiment of the principle put forth in the story of the prodigal son, which Cayce said was basic to the concept of the cycle. In scientific terms, one might well relate this form to the idea of the curvature of space and time, as well as the law of conservation of energy.

While one might like to follow the study of simple geometric forms further and to search for other laws relating to them, it might be of greater interest to look at the atoms of the elements of which the earth is composed. Though individual atoms are too small to be seen, enough is known about them to classify the elements according to the periodic table[6] as well as according to their usefulness. Even a short study of the development of the

---

[6]The periodic table can be described as the chemical table illustrating the periodic system, in which the chemical elements are arranged in order of their atomic numbers.

periodic system will reveal that the elements were originally classified according to periodic law and that the existence of elements missing from the table was predicted on the basis of the certainty of the law governing each element's properties (that is, their expressions). The mathematics of the law involved calls for cyclic manifestations. While it might be argued that the elements operate by mathematical law and that there are no other laws involved, we should consider the usefulness of two of the elements which Cayce described as expressing through laws other than just mathematical ones: He said that gold is a *renewing* force, while silver is a *sustaining* influence. (281-27) Certainly, in the healing arts gold has proved itself to be a renewing force (as seen, for example, in the beneficial effect that gold foil has when it is applied to burns), and the use of silver in photography demonstrates that element's sustaining properties. If gold renews and silver sustains, can it not reasonably be expected that each of the other elements bears a similar function of expression in addition to its mathematical structure? And are not these functions, like the laws manifested in the simple geometric forms, expressions of a more universal language? The following excerpt from the readings indicates that this may be so.

For . . . everything in motion, everything that has taken on materiality as to become expressive in any kingdom in the material world, is *by* the *vibrations* that are the motions—or those positive and negative influences that make for the differentiation that man has called matter in its various stages of evolution into material things.[7]   699-1

From this reading we can see that the atoms, acting with the mathematical precision dictated by the laws governing material expression, gather together in the appropriate forms and relationships to reflect the various concepts man becomes aware

---

[7]"For it enters and it passes through. For . . . all vibration must eventually, as it materializes into matter, pass through a stage of evolution and out. For it rises in its emanations and descends also. Hence the cycle, or circle, or arc, that is as a description of all influence in the experience of man." (699-1) "For . . . all vibration must . . . pass through a stage of evolution . . ." Can this be applicable to those vibrations we send to each other day to day, which we in turn meet as karma (manifested) in others? If so, then the *spirit* in which we treat others passes "*through* a stage of evolution and out"—back to its Maker; thus the shadow we call karma is actually a manifestation of the universal law of projection into and out of matter, the Law of Evolution.

of in the manifested world.[8] Thus it is possible for man to use these forms to become aware of the laws being expressed, so that he can come to understand and use the *laws* rather than being caught up in the utility of things, or manifested forms. And this learning may be accelerated if he is able to comprehend the essences behind the forms. An idea of how these essences or forces work at the atomic level may be gained from this passage:

Q-8. . . . what is meant by the three different vibrations, back and forth, side, and circular?
A-8. These are as the *fundamental forces* of vibration as it applies to the material and spiritual forces in all activities that *become magnified* in a material plane. [Author's italics]   281-6

Here, too, is the concept that basic forces or principles *take form* in materiality so that man can become consciously aware of them. Thus we can see that, rather than being just a useful substance, the atomic world is an expression of universal laws.

Another point of interest is that reading 699-1 contains a clue that might well account for the "atomic life" of the different elements, which generally seems to be viewed as just one of those facts of nature that is yet to be explained. This clue lies in the phrase, "matter in its various stages of evolution," which can be related to the varying atomic lives of the elements. It seems that up to now science has only noted the breaking down of the elements, their rapid or slow deterioration—their atomic life. If the possible evolution of matter is not considered, it would seem that the universe exists as the result of a "Big Bang" type of creation and the atomic clocks thus created are merely running down.

It is now known that what we refer to as atoms are in fact composed of atomic particles, the *forms* of which yet elude direct observation by man. These particles—the real atoms spoken of by

---

[8]The idea expressed here, that atoms carry *information,* is contrary to Werner Heisenberg's statement that "while atomic physics can explain all properties of matter accessible to our senses such as properties of solids, chemical regularities, etc., it is clear that no such *sense properties* can be attributed to the ultimate 'bricks' of matter in a simple way." In a statement that has implications somewhat in contradiction to this, Heisenberg says, "The scientist must reconcile himself to the idea of directly linking the fundamental concepts on which his science rests with the world of his senses." He goes on to say, "The objective world is a product of our active intervention," which ties in with later sections of this presentation.

the Greeks—are the ones we are interested in, for "by the vibrations that are the motion" they express the natural laws of the universe in manners not yet found by man. The only clue that these particles do other than just form the building blocks of the natural elements is found in the Edgar Cayce readings.

The Triangle as a Reflection of the Trinity
Throughout the Manifested Universe

In the preceding few pages we have considered the following possibilities: that all material things are merely reflecting truths promulgated by that Mind which created all; that they do so via the forms of the various atomic structures (the elements); that the triangle is basic to all manifestations in materiality; and that this fundamental role of the triangle is the predicate for the fact that there are only three primary colors in the pigments. At this point it might seem that the roots we have been following in the forest are all leading in different directions; there might even be some doubt that they are parts of the same plant. But in this section as we trace these roots farther, we will find that they are indeed connected and that in joining they form one of the major supports of our tree. To establish connection, let us look at the essence of that simplest of atoms (in the Greek sense of the word)—the atomic particle—and investigate the relationship between the triangle and the three primary colors in an effort to identify the three fundamental concepts necessary for any material manifestation. It is hoped that by doing so we will get a glimpse of the *reality* behind the shadow.

In trying to explain his theory of relativity, Albert Einstein used the image of an elevator moving up or down in empty space.

As an illustration that will suit our purpose, let us use a single atom—there being no other material in the universe. We, in observing that atom, have no body; we are only a mind. The question is, how can we find our relationship to that atom, or its relationship to us? Remember the line we mentioned in our discussion of positive and negative vibrations; how did you draw it—from where to where? The fact is, no line could be drawn from one single atom, for there is no other reference point to determine the direction or length of the line. In order for the single atom to have any meaning, even to the mind that made it, it must be separated from its maker. Thus it is necessary to have a second

28

point, the position of the maker or observer. Now that we have two points, we can speak of the separation between them; but can we, as observers located at one of the points, determine our relationship to the other?

A   B
.   .

To the reader looking down at this page, it might seem that the relationship between points A and B is clearly established; they are a certain distance apart, and the direction from A to B can be meaningfully described. But remember, you are occupying a third position, looking at two other atoms. If you were located at point A, observing point B (there being no other atoms in the universe), what could you tell about the relationship? In the first place, there is no way you could determine distance, for with no other point for comparison any idea such as "near" or "far" would be completely nonexistent. Similarly, you could never describe the direction B lies from A, for without a third point of reference how could there be any concept of up or down, right or left?

As can be seen, no meaningful relationship can be defined between two points alone. Only if there is a third atom can the length and direction of the lines between the points (for now there are three lines to be drawn, not just one) be determined. It is the *direction* of the lines between the three atoms that presents to us the idea of *separation*, and in this process a triangle is formed. Thus it takes three atoms, or points of reference—a triangle—to establish any meaningful relationship in the manifested universe.

But what is this triangle a shadow of? What is the essence behind its form? Is it not a reflection of the Trinity making a point of manifesting Itself in a way that man can perceive? It is surely derived from the Father moving to create something that, when separated, brings into being a *point of reference*, the atom. In other words, here we have the *spirit*, or energy (the Father), moving according to the *idea* (the Son) of forming atoms or *points of reference* for the *purpose* of manifesting itself as Being—the I AM THAT I AM. Hence the Father is manifested via a process of creation that reflects the Trinity in all things, and these three concepts—spirit, idea, and purpose—are the *essence* of the simplest atom, *through which the Creator is revealed throughout the material universe.*

It might be helpful now to bring together some of the main concepts presented so far. As a starting point we can take the readings' statement that "each thought of the Creator bore within itself its *own* fruit as from the beginning" (262-78), which connotes the existence of *separated* manifestations of God; this idea is also implied in reading 262-55, which refers to "those forces...condensed in form to be called matter...." These forces, or spiritual truths—expressions of the Creator—take form in geometric figures, which reflect light (understanding). So we can see that light reflected from material forms carries information that presents spiritual truths, and color is the means through which we can perceive the *essences* of manifested forms. The different shades and hues, like the various atomic structures, reflect variations of the truths presented.[9] Thus the spiritual principles behind all material things, the process of creation and manifestation, the Law of Oneness and the Law of Separation— all can be comprehended through internal reflection on that which casts its shadow as color.

We have not left our study of vibration. What we have done is to examine the atomic world in order to gain an idea of what a vibration is. The force that creates an atom is the same as that which creates a vibration, and since the basic essences of all manifestation are one, an atom and a vibration are merely different shadows of the same unmanifested essence.[10] Therefore, like the atom, a vibration can be defined as follows: A vibration is *spirit moving according to the idea of presenting its purpose.*[11] Another way of phrasing this definition is to say that a vibration

---

[9]The periodic table and spectroscopic analysis illustrate the relationship between form and color. It is interesting to note that, just as there are three primary colors in the pigments, we have identified three essences behind all material manifestations. The correspondences between these three colors and the essences of spirit, idea and purpose will be considered in the next few pages.

[10]For confirmation that an atom and a vibration have the same essential qualities, consider the following excerpt from the readings: "In the development in eternity's realm, is that a finite force as made of creation may become one with the Creator, as a unit, atom, or vibration, becomes one with the universal forces." (900-16)

[11]It is my opinion that a correlation could be made here with Einstein's theory that $E=mc^2$.

is a composition of spirit, idea and purpose, with its specific characteristics depending upon what idea and *what purpose* need to be manifested or comprehended.

The Primary Colors as Shadows of the Essences Behind all Material Manifestations

We have seen that spirit, idea and purpose are the three essences of all manifestation; likewise, it has been noted that in the pigments there are three primary colors—red, yellow and blue—which can be combined to produce any of the various hues that we perceive. At this point we should ask why these three colors are the ones from which all the others are derived. In an effort to answer this question, let us look at the specific relationships between these colors and the three basic essences. It is easy to associate red with energy or spirit, and most people can readily accept this correspondence. Yellow has traditionally been associated with idea, or mind, in many of the ancient writings; but aside from this, there is a reason for this association which must await presentation and clarification until we come to the section of our study dealing with the relationship between vibration and the endocrine system. With red relating to spirit and yellow to idea, blue can be attached only to purpose. That these are not just arbitrary assignments of the colors will become more evident later, but for the present the important item to note is that we are now ready to begin associating specific colors with the essences they enable us to comprehend. Remember, color is vibration, and it is the *only* vehicle via which man comprehends anything through the five senses of his physical body.

So far we have derived these relationships between color and essences:

Red is associated with *spirit.*
Yellow is associated with *idea.*
Blue is associated with *purpose.*

It is hoped that the ideas presented up to this point have made it clear that the implications of these colors are more meaningful and far-reaching than viewing colors merely as different rates of vibration would lead one to expect. As we proceed, it will become evident that the remaining colors of the rainbow also have a much greater importance than is obvious at first glance, for they are the shadows of principles that can lead to an understanding of how and why man comprehends anything at all. These principles—in time, space and patience—are the topic of our next chapter. It is quite possible that our investigation into the principles behind the colors will have the effect of revealing to us that it is through vibration that we discover a bridge *between the material world and God.* This bridge man comprehends via color; when he understands that the colors are but shadows of the essences of all things, he may come to comprehend that bridge.

Summary

While from the very first this chapter seems to digress into a discussion of Newton's theory of light versus Goethe's, the divergent ideas of these two men form the foundation of the concepts presented herein and are necessary for a comprehension of the remainder of this treatise. Newton's work in this field, which dealt largely with spectroscopy and the different vibratory rates of the prismatic colors, is the basis for our postulate that through their rates of vibration the colors bring us information of various contents; and Goethe's theories on the intrinsic value of each color have contributed to our formulation of the concept that the colors are in fact shadows of essences of the creative forces. Combining the ideas of these two theorists led us to a discussion of why there are only three primary colors in the pigments, which in turn led to a consideration of the essences of the material world and, finally, to our definition of a vibration. Here are some of the most important points we touched along the way:

1. On the material level, all the building blocks of the manifested universe are, in their essence, *formed separated* expressions of the mind of the Creator. Man's very existence depends on the Law of Separation, for it was operative in the original creation of souls.

2. In the initial creation God moved, and in that movement was expressed the *all*—the entire universe, but not separated into individual manifestations. Cayce tells us that "all force is one force" and "all life is one life." Therefore, there should be a common denominator—which we have identified as vibration—to every thing and every atom that exists.

3. All matter is the result of creative forces being condensed into forms that we can comprehend. The readings express this

idea in these words: "... all one sees manifest in a material world is but a reflection or a shadow of the real or the spiritual life." (262-23) Thus, every object, atom and vibration is but a shadow of a spiritual force or principle, and it is through the essences of these material manifestations, not their forms, that we can come to comprehend the principles that are being expressed.

4. When light falls on an object it is reflected to us, carrying information about the object we would not otherwise be able to obtain. Therefore—since vibration is light, and light can be defined as understanding—we are continuously using vibrations to find out about the material universe. In fact, this entire presentation would be meaningless if we failed to accept the idea that light carries information.

5. As the readings tell us, "matter is an expression of spirit in motion" (262-78); therefore, we can say that atoms gather together in the appropriate forms and relationships to manifest the spiritual concepts of which man needs to become aware. Since the establishment of any meaningful relationship in the manifested universe requires three points of reference, the triangle (which reflects the Trinity) is the form basic to the geometry of the atomic world. From these observations we were led to the conclusion that an atom is the result of *spirit*, or energy, moving according to the *idea* of forming points of reference for the *purpose* of manifesting itself in materiality.

6. The preceding concept, when considered in connection with the idea that vibrations and atoms, as manifestations of the same creative force, have the same essential qualities, leads us to the central definition of this whole treatise: *A vibration is spirit moving according to the idea of presenting its purpose.*

7. The triangle's being the fundamental form in the atomic world was identified as the predicate for the fact that there are only three primary colors in the pigments. These three colors can therefore be seen as the shadows of the three essences behind all material manifestation. In other words, through their various vibratory rates the colors bring us information about each of these essences. Thus we suggested that:

Red conveys information about the *spirit* (energy) in motion, so that *yellow* can enable us to grasp the *idea* being presented, and through *blue* we can understand the *purpose* for which the spirit moved in the first place.

33

While the postulate that the most elemental atom (or atomic particle) is energy moving according to the idea of manifesting a point of reference may or may not be of paramount importance to the physicist, it is of great significance to our study, especially when we bear in mind that all things are vibration. Certainly one can see how points of reference are relevant to geometric figures and the various atomic particles. The main concept derived from these considerations is that the atomic world brings us information about universal laws; various atoms moving in different geometrical configurations present the various relationships of one law to another. Thus the entire material universe is vibrations moving according to the idea of manifesting their purposes!

Chapter Three
TIME, SPACE AND PATIENCE

It might be tempting now to gather a few roots from the forest and go home, for in arriving at a definition of vibration we have discovered the smallest root. But did we ever look up at the trees which could not exist except for the roots? Can we really say that since we have found a definition for a vibration we need look no further in our study? What about the different forces that cause the variations among types of trees? And what of those that give rise to different kinds of vibration—or is there more than one such force? Does it matter? Remember, just knowing the composition of a vibration does not explain its function, any more than examining the roots of a tree will reveal what that tree is for. It is only by investigating the uses of vibration that we can come to understand our definition of it.

We started this study with questions. It may seem that our inquiry has left us with more unanswered questions than answered ones, even though we have traced the path of color and vibration back to creation, where seemingly it all began. One might feel that we have traveled too many pathways in our effort to explain the essence of a vibration, but it may well be that this is necessary if we are to understand our insufficiencies well enough to be able to comprehend the *why* of vibrations, let alone their usefulness and importance to us. Is it not our insufficiencies that cause the difficulties we have with each other and with life as a whole? In fact, if we can but accept it, it is our very imperfection that is at the root of all our efforts to understand anything at all—ourselves, the world, vibrations, and even God. But this will be dealt with later, for we have looked at only a few of the tools we have for comprehending ourselves.

So far in our study we have considered the following ideas: that we use our five senses in order to gain the essences of things, rather than their shadows, and this we do via color; that in the original creation there were brought into being certain laws or principles necessary for the world to manifest; and that these principles are in reality but tools which, once properly understood, may be used to gain concepts of ourselves that can help us transcend our worldly attachments. According to Edgar Cayce, three of these tools (besides vibrations) are time, space and patience.

That these principles are directly related to our study of vibration should by now be apparent, for we have heretofore noted that they came into existence along with the creation of the material universe:

In this light came creation of that which in the earth came to be matter; in the spheres about the earth, space and time; and in patience it has evolved through those activities until there are the heavens and all the constellations, the stars, the universe as it is known—or sought to be known by individual soul-entities in the material plane. 3508-1

Thus patience is an *active force* (262-26) operating in conjunction with time and space throughout the universe which is "sought to be known" by man. In the Bible we find the expression, "In patience possess ye your souls." (Luke 21:19) Is it any wonder, then, that man seeks to find the answer to time? to space? to patience?

Man, in general, realizes that he is in a three-dimensional world; yet science, while recognizing time and space as two of the three, seeks the third in some sort of space-time continuum which in itself is multidimensional. It may well be that this continuum is what Cayce calls patience, but it is not seen as such by science. In this treatise patience is treated as an active force—separate, yet one with what we call space and time; for it will be shown that these three are but the activative principles inherent within vibrations—the influences which, it is hoped, cause man to seek his relationship to his Maker.

We could stop here, as far as time, space and patience are

concerned, saying merely that they are the activative principles within vibrations, but who would know what was meant by this? We need to study each—time, space and patience—separately in order to gain a comprehension that may be not only meaningful but also directly applicable to further understanding. Before attempting to tie them to the concepts of the atomic forces, let us examine some of Edgar Cayce's statements relative to time, space and patience.

Know, all time is one—as is space, as is patience. 2012-1

You are *in* same (that is, all time as one time), yet become gradually aware of it; passing through, then, as it were, God's record or book of consciousness or of remembrance; for meting, being measured out as it were to that to which thou hast attained. 5755-1

For as time and space and patience in a three-dimensional world are *as* manifestations of truth into the experiences of souls of men... 1463-1

When was the beginning? First consciousness! There is no time, there is no space. Hence the injunction, first know thy spiritual purposes. 2925-1

For with the subconscious forces, we find that called the *measure* of space and time disappears, and the necessity is for a material life to divide such into units called time and space. [Author's italics] 137-8

Yet, as one finds self as a shadow, or as a representative of that indicated in the eternal—one may ask, what is the source of this association or connection?
It is time, space and patience that bridges that distance. These are man's concept of the spirit of God manifesting to the three-dimensional consciousness. 2771-1

For to the entity—as to the world—patience is the lesson that each soul must learn in its sojourn through materiality. And this is a thought for the entity: Time, space and patience are in the mental realm the same as implied by the expression "Father-God, Son and

Holy Spirit," or as Spirit, Body, Soul. They are expressions of the three-dimensional thought.

And in patience then does man become more and more aware *of* the continuity of life, of his soul being a portion of the Whole; patience being the portion of man's sphere of activity in the finite being, as time and space manifest the creative and motivative force.

1554-3

Remember ... to him that was given a measure, as a mete, as a rod to measure heaven—as to how large his heaven would be. All right! Then we have as to how much time—What is time? Is it a record merely of the events of self or of the glory of God? ... This is as a reckoning. Yet as is shown by the indication of so many days...materiality to set (as was said of John) metes and bounds..."

281-33

Let us look more closely at a few chosen phrases in the above quotations that may relate not only to the subject of time and space, but also to other concepts already covered.

... for meting, being *measured* out ... to that to which thou hast attained. [Author's italics]

5755-1

... time and space and patience ... are AS *manifestations* of *truth*... [Author's italics]

1463-1

... the *measure* of space and time disappears, and the necessity is for a material life to *divide* such into units called *time and space*. [Author's italics]

137-8

... one finds self as a shadow, or as a *representative* of that indicated in the eternal ...
These are *man's* concept of the *spirit of God* manifesting ... [Author's italics]

2771-1

Particular attention should be given to 281-33 which seems to characterize time as "the *indication* [as well as the ability]...to *set*... *metes and bounds*" [Author's italics] upon concepts—from which we judge other concepts. We shall meet all the above ideas again as we move forward.

Although these excerpts are just a sample of the total number

38

of comments about time and space found in the Cayce readings, they certainly provide more than ample reason for continuing our study of vibration and its uses, as we attempt to gain a better understanding of our simple definition of a vibration. A first observation about the concepts expressed in these quotations might well be that, in their number and the complexity of their interrelationships, they remind us of the roots in our forest. But, as we will soon discover in our effort to relate time to vibration, these concepts are no more numerous or confusing than the different measurements of kinds of time.

The Essence of Time

Considering the many different kinds of time and their ramifications could easily cause us to become lost in the forest of our roots. Among these various kinds of time we could list: local time, mean time, day-time, temporal time, solar time, sidereal time, psychological time, and atomic time, to name but a few. These terms are really only tools used to describe units of experiences by which man measures movements of one kind or another, and so all of them are directly related to space. Can they be related to patience as well?

Philosophical discussions of time have been well recorded throughout literature. Though these discussions are fascinating and appropriate to our study, because of their immense range, a detailed investigation of them must be left to the reader inclined to follow such. The same applies to the writings of those physicists and mathematicians who have labored throughout the ages to determine the meaning of time, which is perhaps the greatest observable mystery, one which all know but none can really grasp. Fundamental to all such discussions, however, is the seeming existence of a past, present and future—a sequence of events, whether in space or in mind. An eternal NOW violates our sense of becoming, of growth and knowing. Basically, it seems, time is directly related to the *when* of man's oldest questions: when, where and why. The when and the where clearly relate to time and space; that the why relates to patience we shall see later. It must suffice here to realize that the measure of time is one thing and its meaning quite another.

According to science, time can be measured in millionths of

seconds. But is this really so? Movements can be measured that accurately by using our yardstick, the clock; but is it not, in fact, only the movement of the shadow of the hands of the clock that is being measured, and not time itself? Is it not possible that here again we are dealing with the "shadow" of time rather than its essence? Certainly it is by the shadow of the earth that we know day and night. Do we not, in like manner, know any object only by its shadow and reflection of light? Would not the shadow of the moon block us off from the light of the stars were it not for the moon's reflection of light from the sun? Do we not really, and figuratively, yet live in caves—having moved from the underground ones to those we build above ground? Let us get out of our caves so that we might focus on the true essence of time; for—despite the numerous kinds of time mentioned above (which arise from the different kinds of movement that are being measured in the effort to define time scientifically)—"All time is one," as the Cayce readings often say.

In writing about time, most authors and theoreticians have concluded that we know time only by measuring, essentially, the clock time between two events; this implies some kind of movement or motion which the human mind instinctively equates with an abstract idea of time. The horologists have abandoned astronomical time in favor of atomic time, that is, the measuring of vibrations within groupings of various atoms, which allows us to determine time in millionths of seconds. The agitation of atomic particles of the cesium atom, when measured, has been used to produce atomic clocks that remain accurate to within one second in 6,000 years. What scientists are really doing is counting vibrations that emanate from artifically stimulated atomic groupings. Each of these groupings maintains an unwavering frequency of vibration distinctly its own. The ammonia molecule vibrates at exactly 28, 870 megacycles per second, while the cesium atom frequency is a constant 9,121 megacycles per second. Is it not logical that each of these unwavering frequencies (which are called signatures) may be dependent upon the particular atom's structure and usefulness? Could this not also relate directly to the construct of the atom, which we arrived at in our search for an understanding of vibration? Are not the scientists, in a sense, following the same pathway back to the vibratory essence of an atom to find, among other things, time?

Since all atoms vibrate at their own individual rates (that is, all are characterized by energy moving in some kind of cyclic motion), we can meaningfully ask whether each one does not have a particular idea—in the sense of a patterned, intelligent ordering—behind it. To be sure, each atom may be related to a central theme (group) of ideas; yet at the core of each there must be one specific idea, or else there would be chaos. It is herein contended that the rate of vibration reflected by any atom is directly related to the central idea expressed in that atom. In other words, the rate of vibration is merely the *shadow* of the idea behind each one.

Thus the measuring of the shadow of an idea that is being manifested is what the mind *abstracts* as time. But since it is based on the measurement of a shadow, can this conception of time be anything but a shadow itself? To find the essence behind it, we must go back one step and focus on the reality that casts its shadow as the movement we are measuring; and this reality, as noted above, is the idea being manifested.[12] Like all other shadows, the atomic movement we observe in our effort to measure what is usually thought of as time is the medium of expression of that which is behind it; so by truly understanding this shadow we can come to a comprehension of the idea manifested in the particular atom. In reality, then, the measurement is not of our understanding of the shadow (the atom's vibratory rate); it is, rather, the measure of our understanding of the idea being expressed.

Perhaps this reasoning will become clearer if we recall that an atom is energy (spirit) moving according to the idea of manifesting a point of reference, which, in conjunction with other such points in geometric form, presents truths, laws, ideas, etc. This brings us face to face with the concept (fact?) that that which is being manifested via the atom is an *abstract thought* (or an *idea*). The thought does not change—only our concepts change as we reflect upon that manifested idea (the atom) *measured* by us as its vibratory rate. The measurement, then, is not actually of the

---

[12]Here we are looking at the ancient Greek concept of the "unthingly nature of a thing."

shadow, but of our *comprehension* of the idea being reflected. Thus time, in essence, may well be defined as follows:

Time: *The measure of our understanding of the idea being manifested.*

The Essence of Space

Now, in order to understand this definition of time more fully, we must of necessity bring in the concept of space; for the definition, standing alone, is similar to our original single point of reference (the atom) in that we cannot get its full meaning except by considering other reference points. Our comprehension depends upon our understanding not only a single idea, but that idea's relationship to us and to other ideas as well. Thus we find ourselves viewing separate ideas relating in various ways to each other and to us, just as we view separated atoms and objects (manifested ideas) in what is usually considered to be space. It might be argued that space is merely the distance between manifested ideas, but, as was the case with time, we find this common definition concerns only the measurement of shadows (physical manifestations) rather than the ideas behind them.

Let us try to keep our effort to define space simple; leave aside atoms for a moment. How does one idea relate to another? How does one law relate to another? How do the three points of our triangle relate to each other? If the three points are fixed, we have a fixed relationship; but if the points are moving (as in an atom), we have constantly changing relationships.[13]

Space, in essence, has nothing to do with the *distance* between objects (that is, between manifested ideas), for, as noted above, this measurement is only the measurement of shadows. To move to the level of the reality behind these shadows, we have to look at the ideas that are being manifested and the relationships between them. Our comprehension of *how* one idea relates to another may well be a better foundation for a definition of space than is the measurement of distance. This seems especially sound when we consider that time and space are inextricably tied together in our consciousness—for we normally measure time by the changing relationships between objects—and this is possible

---

[13]This point relates to Lewin's theory of relationships, which is part of the study of topology, the branch of mathematics that deals with continuing relationships without regard to magnitude or distance.

only because of our relationship to the objects. Perhaps a meaningful definition of space, then, might be expressed in the following way:

Space: *The measure of understanding of the relationship between manifested ideas.*

Internal and External Definitions of Time and Space

One idea differs from another only as we conceive of differing activities related to them, and their differences are seen only because of the manifestation of that original Law of Separation. We use the Law of Separation, as well as the Law of Reflection, in the gaining of ideas of relationships of any nature. This is true whether we are considering relationships between ideas that are only in our minds or those between ourselves and objects outside us. In both cases, internal and external, we are of necessity dealing with mental concepts. Thus, since both time (as the measure of understanding of an idea) and space (as the measure of understanding of the relationships between ideas) concern single ideas and their relationships to other ideas, the two are manifestly tied together, though they are separable in our awareness. Perhaps we will be able to comprehend better how time and space can be separable yet directly linked to each other if we compare internal definitions of them (definitions of them as they relate to unmanifested ideas within the mind) to the external ones given above. Let us take the following as our internal definitions:

Time: The measure of understanding of an idea.

Space: The measure of understanding of a manifested idea.

Now watch closely as we transpose these definitions relating to the inner, nonmanifest world into ones that take into account external manifestations.[14] Such a comparison is important, for testing two ideas in conjunction with each other helps us to understand each one. We cannot comprehend one idea—cannot know its full range—unless we consider it in relation to all other ideas. Remember, our external definitions were:

Time: The measure of understanding of a manifested idea.

Space: The measure of understanding of the relationships

---

[14]This difference between the internal and external perspectives coincides with and in fact helps to elucidate the disparity between Goethe's work and that of Newton.

between manifested ideas.

In moving from an inner, nonmanifest world to an outer, manifest one (have we here a concept of the Being/non-Being relationship?), we have seemingly violated our earlier definitions of time and space, for the internal definition of space becomes the external one for time. In reality, though, the two sets of definitions are necessary, for one concerns the inner self and the other the inner self's relationship to and comprehension of the manifested world.

In comparing our two definitions of time, we must bear in mind that, since we of necessity comprehend only our inner world, the idea being manifested stands on its own regardless of the form its manifestation takes. Therefore, the more inclusive definition is:

Time: *The measure of understanding of an idea.*[15]

Similarly, let us look at our definitions of space. As we have noted heretofore, any manifested idea can be comprehended only in relationship to other manifesting ideas (remember our triangle), so it is necessary to compare any manifestation with another as a total manifestation. Hence a *difference between* manifestations is inherent in the conceptualization process, which means that the "relationship between manifested ideas" stated in the external definition is implied in the internal one as well. Thus, for space we have this simple yet all-embracing definition:

Space: *The measure of understanding of a MANIFESTED idea.*

The Essence of Patience

So far we have discussed time and space enough to arrive at a definition of each, but we have put off formulating a definition of patience, for we are dealing with a concept of patience that is espoused, as such, only by Edgar Cayce. Here we are faced with a

---

[15]Here we are reminded of Priestly's concept that time is three-dimensional (see *Man and Time,* by J.B. Priestly). Indeed, it cannot be otherwise, for if we recall that each materially manifested idea is composed of the three essences (spirit, idea and purpose), it will be seen that there are three elements of time which must be comprehended. Since none of them can be materially manifested without the others, they are intrinsically bound together in their manifestation, and each must be comprehended. Because of the Law of Separation (manifested separately as space), however, it seems there are three dimensions to time. Is it not possible that in fact we see the three elements as one and yet separately?

question that must be answered before we can continue our discussion: Was Edgar Cayce right in calling our third dimension patience? Furthermore, if he was right, how does this idea tie in with a study of vibration? A starting point in trying to answer these questions is the dictionary, which gives the following as a definition for patience: Calm and uncomplaining endurance, as under pain, provocation, etc.; calmness in waiting; quiet perseverance.

This definition seems to fit the general concept of what patience is. But let us look at some passages from the readings in which the term *patience* is used in a different way.

For, while time and space are literal only to the consciousness of the finite mind, they are a part of the experience in materiality; and the presentations of same then should be of the creative forces—as time, space, patience.

For with the creating of these came the consciousness of being separated from Creative Forces, or God. 2000-3

For to the entity—as to the world—patience is the lesson that each soul must learn in its sojourn through materiality.

... And in patience then does man become more and more aware *of* the continuity of life, of his soul being a portion of the Whole; patience being the portion of man's sphere of activity in the finite being, as time and space manifest the creative and motivative force.

1554-3

Each soul, each entity makes upon time and space—through patience recording same—that as may be indeed the record of the intent and purposes, as well as the material manifestations of the entity through its sojourn in materiality. 1681-1

Thus ye find as ye interpret Father, Son, and Holy Spirit—and bring it into reality, ye pass in time, in space—through *patience*— into the awareness of the other consciousnesses, the other phases of experience of self and of those about thee. 3188-1

Learn again patience, yet persistent patience, active patience— not merely passive. Patience does not mean merely waiting, but as it does for those that would induce nature to comply with nature's laws. So with patience, comply with patience' laws ... making thy daily problems as real as real life—experiences, purposeful in every way. 1968-5

In our opinion, there appears in the above quotations certain key words and phrases relating to the *activity* of patience, as it should be applied, so as to give such an understanding that we may link patience with time and space in a most meaningful manner. Let us focus for a moment on these key phrases:

Reading 1554-3 presents patience as a *lesson* relating to time and space as they manifest the creative and motivative forces. The excerpt quoted above also indicates man's responsibility for patience as an active force: ". . . patience being the portion of *man's sphere* of activity in the finite being . . ." [Author's italics] Note that time and space are characterized as natural forces outside man ("the creative and motivative force"), while patience is an entirely internal activity, one not manifested outside man.

1681-1 tells us that through patience each entity makes *upon* time and space a record of its *intent and purpose*.

According to 3188-1, in time and space we pass into awareness, *through* patience. And this patience, as we find in 1968-5, is *active—not* merely waiting.

Considering these excerpts, are we too far afield in believing that patience is an *activity* related to the *lesson* comprehended in time and space? If this is true, then our activity, in patience, can only be that predicated upon how well we have learned the lesson presented. We would by *active* patience induce nature to comply with nature's laws, and patience with its laws. But, along with ideas, laws and lessons, nature presents *purposes*. How well we comprehend those purposes and by our reactions show that we understand them seems to be the *measure* of that activity Cayce has called patience. *How* we comply with patience' laws will be discussed later.

In reading 2000-3 we find that via time and space we are presented the activity of the creative forces. Earlier we noted that, in the material world, spirit in motion according to some idea reflects the purpose of that movement. (If this were not so, why would the movement exist at all?) And this purpose is inherent within all things. According to this reading, it seems that the awareness of being separated from God can be realized only through time, space and patience. Whether this is very pertinent to our presentation will be determined as we move along.

The next passage, while given as part of a life reading (1554-3) for a specific individual, states as general truth that "patience is the lesson that each must learn in its journey through materiality." Here there is described a "need to learn" directly tied to the manifested world. Can this have any meaning other than that there must somehow be tied to the manifested world a "something" through which we all must learn patience? Would this mean that by just putting up with the material world—enduring it long enough—we could or would come to know patience? If so, would not this passive passage through time and space violate the concept of *active* patience expressed in 1968-5? Also, can we overlook the progress of the soul, or its consciousness, indicated in the phrase "become...aware of the *continuity* of life"? (1554-3) Does this not imply a growth of awareness, of consciousness?

This passage does not, however, necessarily imply a continuity of growth of awareness—only of life. Do we not repeat an experience again and again until we somehow find, or determine, that we no longer must do so? Is it possible that we are caught in the idea of the experience until we accept its purpose, then, and only then, to move on to another? And might not the reason for this needed repetition of the first experience be that until we comprehend its purpose we cannot adequately conceive the subsequent experience? This process of completing one stage before moving on to the next seems natural to the growth of a tree; why would it not be so with other experiences? Would this not be directly in line with the injunction to "induce nature to comply with nature's laws [and] patience . . . with patience' laws"? (1968-5) An affirmative answer to the above questions would, it seems, be a predicate for a crucial concept expressed in 1681-1, that "each entity makes upon time and space—through patience recording same . . . the record of the intent and purposes, as well as the material manifestations . . ."

How does one record that which he does as he moves through materiality, or is there an angel or judge somewhere that records our activities? Is it not we who, so to speak, chalk up our good and bad marks? Is it not we who choose our next activity when one is completed? Would not any other judgment than ours violate the law of free will? If these last three questions can be answered affirmatively, would it not mean that our memory of achievement—that is, our awareness of the purpose of an experience—would be our predicate for an approach to further awareness? And would not the awareness gained from one experience be the basis of our reaction to the new experience? If so, then it is *we* who chalk up the marks of our successes and failures, and the statement in 1681-1 that we make "upon time and space" our own record becomes meaningful; but this process entails our *accepting* and *using* the purpose of any manifestation we are confronted with, for this—the acceptance of our involvement with that manifestation—is a vital part of our awareness of our own progress. In this way there is produced "the record of the intent and purposes, as well as the material manifestations of the entity ..." (1681-1) Thus it is our *doing*, with understanding, which *becomes* that record, that *impression* upon our awareness.

It will become evident that our efforts to comprehend what the readings say about patience have been worthwhile if we read again the excerpt from 3188-1: "... ye pass in time, in space—through *patience*—into the awareness of the other consciousnesses, the other phases of experience of self ..." Here may well be the essence of what patience is—at least that essence which seems necessarily to follow from our definitions of time and space.

It might be well now to review the exact wording of the above passages from 1681-1 and 3188-1 in relation to 1968-5: "Learn again patience, yet persistent patience, active patience ... making thy daily problems as real as real life—experiences, purposeful in every way." Consider how our fuller understanding of patience follows from our definition of time; and consider, too, the indication in these readings that just as patience must be *active*, so time and space are active.

Let us examine the above concepts in connection with our original proposition that any material manifestation is composed of spirit acting out an idea for a purpose. As indicated in reading 3188-1, "... ye *interpret* Father, Son, and Holy Spirit..." Yet it is up to *us* to interpret these manifestations. Is it not how well we interpret that becomes the measure of our awareness? Must we not use the idea, and in some spirit, before we can grasp the purpose? Does not, then, active patience mean *trying* to comprehend a purpose? Do we not test an idea in various relationships (space) before we can fully know its purpose? If so, our interpretation of the purpose would be a *measure* of our awareness.[16] A definition for patience, then, may well be expressed as follows:

Patience: *The measure of understanding of the purpose of a manifested idea.*

The Relationship Between Time, Space and Patience

Thus for time, space and patience we have in our definitions a trinity, and yet the three are in essence one—even as the Father, Son and the Holy Spirit are one. The three are measures of comprehension; yet because each is manifested separately, each must be defined and comprehended separately. These three are given us by the grace of God as tools for measuring not only our abilities, but also our progress toward becoming one with God. This idea will be developed later.

We have noted above that time and space are inextricably and essentially tied together by reason of the Law of Separation. There is another reason for their being connected, which should be noted here, before we look more closely at our definition of patience. For patience too is related to time and space as we know them, but we rarely notice this to be so.

Consider for a moment just how we might know time if the universe were not in motion through space. There would be no days or nights, no clocks, no growth, no life or death—no movements at all to measure. Time would not seem to exist; but would space? (Here we come to the idea, so often considered, that there may really not be a sound unless there is someone to hear it; but this question, though related to vibrations, is outside the context of the present study.) It might be argued that to an observer who could take in the whole panorama at one glance, without movement of consciousness, space certainly would exist. But would there be any reason to measure the differences between the objects seen, or even to become aware of their existence? If we consider this question, it may readily be conceded that time and space are directly relative to each other, but the connection with patience might not necessarily be seen. We equate time with movement and space with distance, in both cases because we notice them. *Why* they are there to be noticed may well be the reason for the dimension of patience.

---

[16]Protagoras said, "Man is the measure of all things."

It might be argued that man is an accident of creation, a development only by reason of the earth's particular environment. But this study, in part at least, must hinge upon the story of creation as expressed by Edgar Cayce (and the Biblical story in Genesis), for these sources at least present a reason for time and space—and even the creation itself—that seems not to be found elsewhere.[17]

It has been noted that the manifested world, at least at the atomic level, presents laws, truths, principles, etc. Yet it might well be that they of themselves are of little value unless they are applied or tested against each other. Within the context of the macrocosm, could it not be that the movements of stars reflect the testing of one principle against another? Might they not present a *lesson*, or at least an experience in creation—even to a creator? And is not each of us a microcosm of the macrocosm, a pattern of the universe? A creator, at least of his own ideas?

At this point it might be well to recall reading 1554-3, which tells us that "...in patience then does man become... aware *of* the continuity of life..." and that through this process he learns that "...lesson that each soul must learn in its sojourn through materiality..." Can this mean other than that man must learn his *lesson* by studying the truth presented by the movement of the universe as we see it? Is it not through these movements (by which we measure time) that we also observe the purpose of it all? Does not observing the processes of creation and destruction enable us to learn and experience the "positive and negative" aspects of creative forces? And is it not evident that time presents the *continuity* of the truths manifested so that we can learn the purposes inherent in the truths? If so, then time and space are predicates for our achieving a goal other than just learning the purposes manifested in the atoms and the total universe. Our observance of the truths presented and our participation in the testing of them is a learning process that determines our involvement with them. *We*, then, are responsible for our material involvements—our creations and destructions. So any conception of patience must include a concept of our involvement

---

[17]The story of creation as found in the Cayce readings and partially quoted herein is a separate study published by the A.R.E. Press. Known as the "Creation Trilogy," the books are entitled *Before the Beginning, The River of Time,* and *You Are Forever.* (Set #100, $4.95)

not only with the material world, but also with the truths and principles presented therein.

An Internal Definition of Patience

Here again we are faced with a definition for patience, relative to our inner world that may seem different from that of patience as it relates to the atomic universe, for the latter definition may or may not reflect our involvement. But when we manipulate the atomic world according to our wishes, when we extract its forces for our use and interfere with the natural evolution of animals and plants, and when this same disregard is evident in our treatment of each other, how can we fail to admit our involvement with the results? If it is true that what we sow we also reap, then surely what happens to us is at least partially caused by us. Can we ultimately avoid accepting our responsibility for what befalls us? Is not the purpose of what happens, at least to the extent that we have caused it, to reflect to us our part in its cause, its creation? If so, then our "sojourn through materiality" (1554-3) has brought us a lesson in creation—if nothing more—and we thus become aware, not only of ourselves as creators, but of our continuity of life.

A natural question arises here as to the part we are playing as creators of the events that happen to us. Are we not learning to *be* creators? Must we not, as Cayce put it, ultimately become co-creators with God? Could we become creators without engaging in creation? And must we not recognize and accept our part in the creation of the situations in which we find ourselves? If so, then our creations must reflect our efforts in like manner as we understand that God's creations reflected His efforts. Could any of us be "one with God" and not be an equal in creative ability, at least in the microcosm? It seems that the answer to our questions must be affirmative, and our definition of patience, at least as it relates to our inner world, might then be more precisely expressed as follows:

Patience: *The measure of our understanding of our responsibility for whatever happens to us; or the measure of our understanding of our responsibility for a manifested idea.*

But are we not just expanding our concept of purpose in order to make it more understandable to us, more palatable and easier to accept? Surely whatever happens to us can have more than one purpose, just as there are more than one idea and purpose in atomic manifestation. So perhaps rephrasing our definitions of time, space and patience so that they can refer to ideas (plural) will further clarify them.

Time: *The measure of understanding of ideas.*

Space: *The measure of understanding of the relationship between manifested ideas.*

Patience: *The measure of understanding of the purpose of manifested ideas.*

The Importance of How We Perceive the Dimensions

Assuming that we can accept these definitions for what they purport to be—just aids to help us grasp the essences of the dimensions—we still must pose the question of why they are even presented here. The answer is evident if it is conceded that time, space and patience are merely tools for our comprehension and are related to spirit, ideas and purposes; for if this is the case, *how* they are perceived as measures is most certainly relevant to our study of vibration.

At this point it might be pertinent to ask what could at first glance be viewed as an impertinent, implausible question: Is it possible that in following the roots of the trees in our forest we are approaching an understanding of the Tree of Life? Although it might seem naive of us to believe this, are we not, as the trail becomes clearer and the root larger, moving toward the concept that the ALL may be expressive via vibration? We certainly would not claim that the ALL can be explained or known; we are merely exploring the possibility that the study of vibration may be the key to recognizing the tree. Surely the idea that "in patience then does man become ... aware *of* the continuity of life" (1554-3) implies a living forever. But this need not belie our concept that physical man is not to eat of the Tree of Life. Rather, it seems to indicate that flesh man is but a shadow of the real; yet the shadow, too, reflects its Maker.

Summary

If the Cayce readings are correct, the subject matter studied in this chapter had its origin in the initial creation, in which certain laws and principles necessary for the universe were brought into being. These principles are in fact merely tools that we can use to gain a comprehension of ourselves, the world around us, and our purpose within it. Among these tools are time, space and patience, which Cayce identified as the three dimensions of the material universe. These three tools are vital to any study of vibration, for they are the activative principles within vibrations that influence man to seek his relationship with his Maker. Thus each is related to awareness, to *understanding;* indeed, they are central to the comprehension process itself. Because of them we are conscious of ourselves as beings, for it is the constant movement of ideas that gives rise to our sense of identity. Here are some of the main concepts we encountered in our investigation of time, space and patience:

1. Time is commonly considered to be the interval between two events, a definition that implies spatial movement of one sort or another. But in measuring time in this way, are we not in fact measuring the movement—the shadow of time—rather than time itself? In an attempt to grasp the essence behind this shadow, we noted the fact that each atom vibrates at a specific, constant rate, and we postulated that this rate is a reflection of the central idea expressed in that type of atom. Since the measure of this vibration is the basis for what is generally thought of as time, it is logical to conclude that in reality time is the measure of the essence behind the atom's vibratory rate (that essence being the idea the specific atom is manifesting). Thus we were led to the following definition:

Time is the measure of our understanding of manifested ideas.

2. Similarly, space is usually thought of as the distance between things (manifested ideas). But here again we are dealing with shadows, for are not material things merely shadows of the ideas they are manifesting? The essence of space, then, lies in the separateness not of things, but of the ideas behind them. From this reasoning we derived this definition of space:

Space is the measure of our understanding of the relationship between manifested ideas.

3. Unlike the dictionary, which defines patience as a type of passive endurance, the Edgar Cayce readings stress "active patience," (1968-5) which is identified as "the lesson that each soul must learn in . . . materiality." (1554-3) But exactly what is it that we must learn through our material experiences? Is it not the purpose behind those experiences? For once we have gained

an understanding of the purpose of one experience, are we not free to move on to and learn from another? Patience, then, might be defined as follows:

Patience is the measure of our understanding of the purpose of manifested ideas.

4. Time and space are clearly related to each other, for if there were no movement through space (for example, no revolution of the earth around the sun, and no vibrations on the atomic level), we would have no means of noticing the passing of time. How these two are related to patience is a bit harder to see, but a little thought will show that there is indeed such a relationship. Remember, any manifestation is the result of spirit moving according to the idea of presenting its purposes. Would it be in any way possible to learn the purpose behind the manifested idea (refer to our definition of patience) without first coming to some understanding of the idea itself (note our definition of time)? And would not testing the idea in relationship to other ideas (recall how we defined space) also be a prerequisite for grasping its purpose? Thus we have in time, space and patience a trinity of principles—each manifesting separately, but each closely interrelated with the others.

Are the roots in our forest getting a bit easier to follow? Do they seem, perhaps, to be leading in the same general direction? Is the connection between vibration, color, and time, space and patience—the tools we use to approach an understanding of the universe and our place in it—becoming somewhat clearer? The concept that we perceive all things as color, and that colors themselves are but shadows of the real, has yet to be related to time, space and patience. The nature of this relationship and its relevancy to vibration will, it is hoped, become more understandable as we delve into the mysteries of the rainbow— the next root we will attempt to trace.

Chapter Four
THE RAINBOW
AND ITS SYMBOLOGY

I do set my bow in the cloud,
and it shall be for a token of a covenant
between me and the earth. Genesis 9:13

The General Symbology of the Rainbow
and the Story of Noah

The story of the flood, as told in the Bible and found in the
mythological writings and legends of most ancient cultures, may
well be more than it seems. Surely one can associate Noah's ark
with the Ark of the Covenant, which in turn is symbolic of the
place of the Most High within. Could it be that each Biblical event
is, at least partially, the outward manifestation of an inner
development, and could the Old Testament be more aptly a story
of man's evolution than is generally recognized?[18] Some
justification for such an assumption may be gleaned from the
answer Edgar Cayce gave in the following passage:

*Q-14. Would the history of the Jewish race from Abraham to Jesus
parallel the development of the embryo from conception to birth?*

A-14. Rather would the history of man from Noah to Abraham,
while that from Abraham to Christ would be the mental
unfoldment of the body. For, that which leads to the Christ is the
mind. And the mind's unfoldment may be that indicated from
Abraham to the Christ.   281-63

---

[18]In this connection, it may well prove worthwhile to study Goethe's "History
of Science" against a background of the history of the human mind. He also
seemed to feel that a history of color theory could well parallel the
development of science, at least from a historical standpoint. That Goethe
caught at least a glimpse of a concept similar to that expressed by Edgar
Cayce could stimulate those interested to follow this parallelism further.

While this reading was given for a group studying the Book of Revelation and its connection with the endocrine system, it seems not awry to take the parallels described as being literally true; that is, we may well believe that the Biblical stories really portray the outward manifestation of man's inner development, of his body and his mental capacities—his evolution through the material world.

It is interesting to note that here Cayce describes man's physical development as starting with Noah rather than Adam.[19] It is reasonable to infer from this that the story of Noah actually concerns the merging of the spiritual creation with the physical. Should this concept be plausible in some fashion, it may well be that the Noah story reveals to us a last Biblical picture of the creative processes. The flood symbolizes that man was subject to being flooded with the emotions, which are represented by the water covering the earth; yet, just as Noah's life was preserved by his entering the ark, man could come to know the certainty of the continuity of life by withdrawing into the *ark* within.

Another aspect of the symbolism in the story of the deluge will be seen if we consider that surely the nature of man's comprehension processes is the same now as it has been since creation. If man now comprehends all things through color, is it not logical to assume that the ability to do so was a natural development in his evolution? Would not the evolving spirit, which projected into matter and thus brought about its "first death," need something to hold to as an item for faith? Surely Noah recognized the rainbow as such, and the Bible clearly identifies it as the symbol of God's covenant with him; but nowhere do we find it stated that the rainbow is a representation of man's comprehension process. Nevertheless, it is possible that the process of comprehension may in fact be a part of what the rainbow symbolizes, for the covenant could concern Noah's recognition of a truth of which he previously had been unaware.

Before we consider the specific colors in the rainbow, let us look at the significance of its design and the sequence of its colors. Its overall circle is the well-known symbol of the *All*, yet normally only the upper half is seen. Could this phenomenon be a symbol to man,

---

[19]This is consistent with other Cayce readings on creation, for here we are discussing man's development after his physical creation. See the "Creation Trilogy" published by the A.R.E. Press.

though for eons unrecognized as such, that the unseen part of the rainbow would be found within himself, hidden in the earth? that it would, in fact—since all perception is based on color—be that through which he would come to know anything at all? Is not the rainbow, then, actually a symbol of the Christ, at least to the undeveloped man? For by his use of color for comprehension, man becomes aware of his separation from God. Thus its use *saves* him from his forgetfulness and his projection into matter.

The Biblical story states it to be a symbol of a covenant of God with man, and can this not be identified with the Christ, which was promised even from the first? Another significance to the rainbow is in the double symbolism of the promise, for, as will be seen as we continue our study of vibration, the hidden, yet manifested savior and the crucifixion are both embodied in it. We will consider this point further in a more appropriate place.

Other significant meanings and symbols are found in the color sequence and in the double and triple rainbows that are sometimes seen. The color sequence—with red on the outside, followed by orange, yellow, green, blue, indigo and violet—can be taken to represent the outward nature of man evolving toward the inner man, for, as we shall see, the progression is toward an inner comprehension of the outside manifested world. Would not this sequence, then, symbolize the evolution of consciousness, of man's mental capacities, from Noah to Christ? This possibility will become more plausible as we study the colors as a medium for comprehension. Some of the symbology of the individual colors will be dealt with later, but at this point we might note that their definite separation can be viewed as an emblem of man's disunion from God, or at least of the principle of separation through which we must become aware of this disunion.

Double and triple rainbows could well symbolize the duality and the trinity that may be found in man. The rainbow most easily perceived would then relate to physical man—that aspect of himself of which he is most readily aware—while the less visible ones would relate to his mental and spiritual natures.

One may wonder at these seeming diversions in our study of vibration, but in fact they are not diversions at all. If we succeed in following the many roots in our forest back to their source, we will ultimately be led to recognize not only their relevance, but their oneness.

The Colors

Let us now give some consideration to the colors of the rainbow. As seen by us, the colors seem to rise in the vibratory scale, starting with red, which we have related to spirit or energy. Thus far we have also considered two others—yellow, which we equate with ideas, and blue, which has been identified with purposes. It has been shown not only that these relate to the atomic world, but that they are *seen* by us so that we can understand the essences of the manifested universe. If we comprehend the spirit (or force) through red, the ideas manifesting as yellow, and their purposes as blue, what of the other colors of the rainbow? Are they as significant and meaningful as the three so far identified?

Referring to the chart below, which shows the correspondences we have already derived, might make it easier to follow the remainder of this section.

COLOR	ESSENCE
Violet	Purpose
Indigo	
Blue	Idea
Green	
Yellow	Spirit (Energy)
Orange	
Red	

In all of this, let us not forget that "color is but vibration... movement . . . of a positive and negative force" and, "there are those forces that move in light, color and sound . . ." It will be shown that there are forces other than those we have considered up to now, and we must examine them if we are to be diligent in our study of vibration. But for the present, let us try to find a primary essence to the other colors in our rainbow.

In the previous chapter, we considered time, space and patience at some length (though there is certainly much more that could be said about them). If it is true that we comprehend all things only via vibration, and that vibration is in fact color, would we not comprehend time, space and patience as color? And if we did so, through which colors would we become aware of them? (Remember the significance of the lower part of the rainbow, the segment hidden in the earth: that we generally are not yet aware that everything is actually perceived via color.) Let us consider how we might arrive at a color relating to time, to space, and to patience. We could, of course, arbitrarily assign a color to each, but this study requires at least a semblance of a reason (a root?) for making such associations. It would seem that the most logical place to look for a key to the colors through which we can comprehend time, space and patience is in the definition of each dimension.

Let us first consider time, which has been defined as the measure of understanding of an idea. According to our hypothesis, any idea is the result of spirit (or energy) manifesting that idea. This means that there is a direct connection or relevancy between the spirit and the idea, regardless of the purpose for the idea's manifestation. This direct relevancy—this *betweenness*—should naturally lead us to identify time's color as being between red (spirit) and yellow (idea).

Perhaps we will be able to see this point more clearly if we consider that our comprehension of the relationship of one manifested (atomic) idea to another is dependent upon the movement of material bodies—such as the earth, moon, stars, and even atoms in vibration—and this movement is what becomes perceived as time. But what we are dealing with at this stage is a movement toward the understanding of an idea, which does not necessarily entail full comprehension. Our starting point is the sensing of just the movement of spirit. This is not time, but a sensing of ideas in possible relationships, which can lead to a sensing relative to our understanding of those ideas. This movement of our consciousness toward full comprehension of the idea itself is perceived as that which we call time. Thus time is literally between the sensing of the movement of spirit (red) and full understanding of idea (yellow), so that its color can most logically be identified as orange.

To look at this question from another angle, consider that atomic vibration is the primary characteristic by which we recognize any manifested idea, for the energy inside the atom must be moving at a rate sufficient to manifest that particular idea (that atom), and this rate must be constant, or the manifestation would change. It seems that all energy, at the atomic level, moves at the same constant rate, for the equation $E=mc^2$ certainly is constant. This *constancy*, which is tied to the energy in motion and the idea being manifested, is perceived by us at the deeper intuitive level as orange and is called time.

Next let us consider space. Again we need to look at our definition: Space—the measure of understanding of a manifested idea; or, the measure of understanding of the relationship between ideas. For the understanding of relationships, which may vary almost immeasurably (remember the variable points of the triangle), there needs to be a mind operating. With the colors discussed to this point, we have dealt only with *constant* manifestation (red, as spirit; yellow, as idea; blue, as purpose; and now orange, as the constant flow or movement of energy—all as related to *manifested* ideas). While the constant energy-flow rate at the atomic level is the same as that in the speed of light, neither can be comprehended apart from its manifestations. Relationships between bodies of manifestations, like the earth, moon and stars, vary in many ways. Such objects can be perceived directly, and though we consciously work with the measurable distances between them as being space, this is in reality just the measure of differences between shadows. Thus space, in essence, concerns the relationships between ideas, either manifested or unmanifested. This real spatial measurement needs to be perceived by us as a constant reality, for inwardly or outwardly we are always aware of constantly changing relationships, whether we understand them or not.

This activity of perception of relationships is not limited to atomic manifestations, as is time, for relationships between mental concepts also must be considered. Space, because it is in reality a *mental* conception of relationships, may be considered above the other principles we have examined, and thus it would appear as a higher color in the rainbow.

Since what we are dealing with here relates to the perception process, it may well be that that which we call space is the outward manifestation of the inward mental activity involved in the constant measuring of relationships. This mental process would be necessary before the purpose of anything could be understood, either partially or fully. Thus the color for space would be closely allied to, but below, that for patience (the measure of understanding of the purpose of an idea), for the measuring of relationships must precede full comprehension of purposes. The only two colors not previously considered that are next to each other in the spectrum are indigo and violet. If the growth is upward, the color for space would be indigo and that for patience would be violet.

We become *aware* of the purpose of any atom (manifestation) through the color blue, we come to comprehend its relationships to other such manifestations via indigo, and finally the *total understanding* is arrived at when we grasp the color violet. The progression of understanding is from the one, to the many, to the total. The sequence of blue, indigo and violet is thus quite meaningful as a trinity in itself, and—when we consider patience as the measure of our understanding of the purpose of manifested man—the reason for relating this dimension to the highest color becomes especially clear.

At this point it may be well to take note of a phenomenon sometimes mentioned by writers about color perception. It has been alleged by some that man has not always perceived color in the manner that modern man does so. It is theorized that in early Grecian times man, as a whole, was not aware of the color blue. Whether or not this is true, this characteristic apparently has a counterpart in some people today, for, it seems, some individuals are aware of only *six* colors in the rainbow, indigo and violet seeming to them to be just one color. This phenomenon could certainly be related to the evolution of the physical and mental faculties of man, as mentioned in reading 281-63 at the beginning of this chapter. It might also have a direct relationship to the fact that animals and birds in some instances are unable to see certain colors, which could indicate that they too are in various stages of development and are not yet fully evolved.[20]

Green

It may seem that we have been avoiding a reference to the color green, for we have noted an essence for each of the three colors below green in the spectrum and for each of the three higher ones. Though the color correspondences derived above might seem

---

[20]Consider Genesis 9:15-16, which states clearly that the covenant symbolized by the rainbow relates equally to man and "every living creature": "And I will remember my covenant, which is between me and you and every living creature of all flesh; and the waters shall no more become a flood to destroy all flesh. And the bow shall be in the cloud; and I will look upon it, that I may remember the everlasting covenant between God and every living creature of all flesh that is upon the earth." (Scofield, Authorized Version)

arbitrary to some, this presentation has sought to demonstrate the logic of the sequence at which we have arrived. We have previously noted that in some respects the rainbow as a whole represents the Christ, a concept that may lead us to a greater understanding of the word *Christ* as it relates to a function within our own lives. Now let us consider the possibility that green specifically may have a special relationship to the Christ.

First, let us look at the symbolism of green's position in the middle of the rainbow. Above green we have three colors, as we do below it; this brings to mind the quotation "as above, so below." It may well be claimed that the three lower colors relate to the conceptualization of the manifested world by the conscious mind, while the higher three relate to cognizance of the spiritual world. In a sense this may be true, but this division may relate more to man's evolutionary process than to the higher and lower minds.[21]

In the beginning of the earth, so to speak, spirit (that is, souls) pushed into matter, thus causing what is called the first death, or man's forgetting of his source. The resurrection from this death is by way of Christ the Savior, represented by that color between the lower and the higher ones, which, as noted above, is green. Certainly Jesus said, "I am the way," and the Christ is generally recognized as man's savior. It is also true that a vertical line drawn through the color sequence of the rainbow and another drawn horizontally through the green area make the sign of the cross, a major symbol for Christ. It would seem, though, that these considerations do not reveal the entire significance of green.

Our search may be more rewarding if we follow Cayce's admonition to help "nature to comply with nature's laws." (1968-5) Let us take a look at nature, for does it not show the handiwork of God? Do we not see green in the growth of the tree whose roots we have been tracing? Is not nature's green all about us? And what is thereby signified to us? Is it not life, and growth—even evolution itself, as the seed evolves into the tree? If so, then does green relate only to growth? Surely growth is recognized by green. But can there be another and more comprehensive meaning to this color?

Remember that the coming of the Savior, the Christ, was

---

[21]A natural question arises here. If the period from Noah to Abraham relates to the development of the physical, and that from Abraham to Jesus the mental, what development does the present period indicate? It seems only logical that it would be that of the spiritual.

promised even from the first, and the "covenant" was signified by the rainbow. Would it be too much to consider that man has an obligation to God's covenant with Noah? Would not the thought "My spirit beareth witness with thy spirit" be a saving factor that comes into effect as we follow the ways of Christ? Does not the evolutionary principle require the shedding of the old to be replaced by the new?

It may well be asked just how this "shedding" of the old is done and how it relates to the principle shown in green. Remember, we have insisted that patience relates to full comprehension of a manifestation, which depends upon our acceptance of our involvement in its creation. Once we have accepted our responsibility relative to what happens, would it not be then, and only then, that growth in consciousness could become a reality? And would this not come about through the shedding of the expressions that caused the happening? Would this not be analogous to the shedding of the leaves of the tree as the tree grows to maturity? It seems that once we accept our responsibility for what happens to us, the Christ Principle saves us from further involvement by bringing us full comprehension of the purpose of the event. It is as if we cannot receive full comprehension until we are ready to shed the previous expressions (leaves); then the Christ Principle activates our comprehension. Perhaps this is the way in which our obligation to the covenant reflected in the rainbow is fulfilled.

Might not green represent that essence behind what we would call growth, change, evolution, and the shedding of the old and putting on of the new, all as one principle? Could the acting out of this principle by us be a fulfilling expression of respect for God's covenant with Noah? Certainly God's promise to Noah was that life would not again be erased from the face of the earth. Could we call this a promise that the "life force" would always remain? And is green not the color most appropriate to symbolize this force? Could green also represent that inherent in the concept "from darkness unto light," and thus relate to the "knowing Principle"—the recognition of consciousness itself, the idea of *Being?*[22] That this last idea may well signify that green holds a

[22]Here we may well be reminded of the positive and negative forces portrayed in the twelfth chapter of the Revelation, in which John beheld "a woman clothed with the sun, and the moon under her feet—and she being with child cried, travailing in birth, and pained to be delivered."

greater meaning than just change, growth or evolution will be noted later, when we discuss the seat of the ego; but if we can give an affirmative answer to the above questions we might say that the principle shown by green may well be summed up in the statement: *Green represents the Christ Principle.*

Remember, there is within every force something that seeks to know its Maker; and would this something not be the *identification* implied in the statement "I and my Father are one"? While some might consider this identification or consciousness to be more acceptable as the essence behind green, it seems that the Christ Principle is more encompassing, as will become especially evident as we study "those forces which move in light, color, sound" in the next chapter.

In our discussion of time, space and patience, we have noted that each is as a "measure." They may be likened to the process of being "weighed in the balance"; as the forces and ideas of the various atomic manifestations are weighed in concert with one another—a process that involves valuation of each in relation to the whole—there is produced the awareness of being one *with* the whole (Christ Consciousness).

Yet perhaps a more meaningful understanding might be found if we look closely at another of the Cayce readings. The following quotation from a reading given on the subject of "Day and Night" point once again to the beginning of creation as the origin of meanings just now coming to our awareness. (This may make one wonder if it is not true that *we* are yet at the beginning, just being awakened; if this is the case, what is time?) This reading is so directly relevant to this study that it is quoted in its entirety in the Appendix; the following portions are those considered important to our search for the essence of green.

... conditions that exist in the material plane are but shadows of the truths in the mental and spiritual plane.

Hence we find, as given, that first there was for matter, that gathered in a directed plane of activity called the earth, the separation of light and darkness.

Hence these, then, are figures of that from the spiritual plane termed in the mental world as the good and evil or in the spiritual as facing the light and the dark, or facing the source of light—which, to the mind of those that seek to know His biddings, is the voice, the word, the life, the light, that comes in the hearts, minds, souls, of each to awaken them, as individuals, to their relationships with the source of light.

Again, in the figurative sense, we find that light and darkness, day and night, are represented by that termed as periods of growth and the periods of rest or recuperation, *through the activities of other influences in those forces or sources of activity condensed in form to be called matter,* no matter what plane this may be acting from or upon. [Author's italics]   262-55

In the same reading, the following answer was given to a question about the words alpha and omega.

Compare this with that written in Isaiah, as to how the Lord, *the God, is the beginning and the end of that brought into material manifestation, or into that known by man as the plane or dimension from which man reasons in the finite.* Then there will be to the body the correct conception of that meant, "I am alpha and omega, beginning and the end." *That God, the Father, the Spirit, the Ohm, is the influencing force of every activity is not wholly sufficient unto man's salvation, in that he is a free will being.* As intimated that alpha, beginning; omega, ending. *For, the confirmation, the segregation, the separation, the building, the adding to it, is necessary—in relation to those activities that lie between—for* man's building to the beginning and the end. [Author's italics]
262-55

In the above passages we find not only mention of the "influences in those forces . . . condensed in form to be called matter," as previously discussed, but the statement that "God . . . is the influencing force of every activity . . ." Can this not well be indicating that green is a manifestation (shadow) of that influencing force which, in the processes of *growth* and *decay,* would picture or exemplify to man the idea that God is the beginning and end of all things, the alpha and omega? Is it not possible that man would, though perhaps unconsciously, recognize the *life force* in nature to be that of "faith," the assurance that God is ever present in the earth?

Thus green symbolizes much more than just evolution, growth, change, or even that which is generally conceived of as the Christ Consciousness; and yet, is there not a Savior implied in the phrase "not wholly sufficient unto man's salvation" because of his free will? And is not the *Savior* model completed in Jesus, who surrendered His will to that same *influencing* force noted above? If so, then the term *Christ Consciousness* as a fulfilling of the thought expressed in "the first shall be last and the last first" might aptly apply to the *Savior* that stands between the spirit force which pushed into matter, and the purpose of it all. It seems that green, which is between the colors that represent these two in the rainbow, might well symbolize that saving force, the Christ Principle.

What exactly does green, as the shadow of the Christ Principle, encompass? Green has been called the healing force, and rightly so in the context of the healing of illness. Yet does not healing require an illness? Would not this aspect of green, then, be an earthly phenomenon rather than a principle? Or suppose that green is love; would this not be a principle? Certainly love is as a principle, but would it not also have been implied in that divine decision, "Let us make man in our image"?

These explorations of concepts might seem superfluous, even metaphysical in argument; yet when we consider that "forces... condensed in form to be called matter," and the attendant influences of those forces, such explorations seem very relevant to man's purpose in the earth.

Before moving on in our study, we must interject a note that might prove upsetting to some. In our earlier discussion of the colors in the spectrum, we observed that there are four primary colors in light, but only three in the pigments. If green represents a "principle" (such as evolution or the Christ Consciousness) and red, yellow and blue represent the principles of spirit, idea and purpose, we would expect these four to be the primary colors in light; but prismatically, this does not work out to be so.[23] Nevertheless, this presentation takes the position that green is in fact a primary color, for, being the shadow of the Christ Principle, it is most certainly present in the atomic world as the "influencing" force (or God!), though not manifest until Jesus, the model for man.

As the chart following shows, the atomic colors red, yellow and

[23]The reader might wish to consult the work of von Kries, who proved that three types of stimulus produce four color sensations; the reason for this phenomenon remains an enigma to science, but further examination might prove it meaningfully related to the ideas presented here.

66

blue represent principles. Time, space and patience, on the other hand, are the activating stimuli to man's consciousness; thus they are not principles, in this sense, but creative activities.[24] The principles of spirit, mind and purpose (red, yellow and blue), when activated by time, space and patience (orange, indigo and violet), produce that ultimate of creation, the Christ Consciousness, which in reality is that principle existent from the beginning: "Let us make man in our image."

COLORS	MATERIAL WORLD	MENTAL WORLD		SAVIOR
	Atomic Manifestations Vibrations	Activating Principles	Consciousness-Evolving Principles	Covenant
Violet		Patience ⟶	Patience ⟍	
Indigo		Space ⟍		
Blue	Purpose			
Green		⟍	Self ⟍	Christ Principle
Yellow	Idea			
Orange		Time ⟋		
Red	Spirit(Energy)		⟋	

Thus, through its form and colors, the rainbow portrays much more than just the promise of no more floods. The colors in the rainbow become higher as they approach the self. As shown in our chart, they first relate to the total material world and its manifested ideas (red, yellow and blue), which, when weighed in the balances of time and space (orange and indigo), brings an awareness of the self (green). The self, not yet recognizing the essences behind the colors (the colors being but shadows), makes choices of actions according to its ideals, which are weighed in their relationships to the self's purposes.

The promise (covenant) is that implied in the justice of the scales, which the self becomes aware of as it weighs its desires against its understanding of its creative efforts. Thus the justice of God is also represented in the rainbow. Through this justice (weighing measures of understanding against desires) the self proves the concept "Thou art weighed in the balances, and art

[24]It may be recalled that our definitions for space and patience both relate to *purposes,* which is the principle represented by blue. Thus, in relation to the purpose of anything, violet, indigo and blue may well be considered as *one* stimulus to the conceptualization processes.

found wanting." (Dan. 5:27) Yet this *weighing* and balancing produces the Savior of the self, as we discover through our experiences that "In your *patience* possess ye your souls." (Luke 21:19)

The *Savior* cannot be produced, however, until the measures of understanding are sufficient to bring the awareness that "I can of mine own self do nothing." (John 5:30) When the self has learned to "Be still, and know that I am God," (Ps. 46:10) the rain (as an outward symbol of grace?) washes the self of its adulteration of the creative forces, and there follows the unadulterated *light* of understanding. The *change* from doing our will to doing God's will produces the *Savior* from self's activities. Hence, though the separation of the rainbow's colors symbolizes our separation from God, its form encircles us with His love so that we might know that we are Sons of God.

Summary

Our study of the rainbow and what it represents has brought us much more than just a knowledge of the separation of light into its component colors. Newton proved that sunlight is a composite of differing rates of vibration that join to produce white light; we have tried to demonstrate that each of those various vibratory rates is the shadow of an essence that can be used as a tool to help bring about our ultimate reunion with our Maker. The following are some of the main points made in our investigation.

1. The rainbow as a whole and the story of Noah are rich in meaning. The story of the flood shows how man, though he may be flooded by his own emotions, can come to know the continuity of life by withdrawing into the place of the Most High (the ark) within. The rainbow itself can be taken as a symbol of man, his comprehension process, and the promised Christ. The separation of its colors reflects man's separation from God; its color sequence is emblematic of the evolution of consciousness; and the unseen half of its circle, hidden in the earth, indicates that the way to man's salvation is at hand, within himself.

2. Each color in the rainbow is the shadow of a deeper essence—a spiritual principle or an activating stimulus. Red, yellow and blue have previously been related to spirit (energy), idea and purpose. By carefully considering our definitions for time, space and patience and seeing how these definitions relate

68

to the sequence of colors in the rainbow, we reached the following conclusions:

Orange reflects *time* as its essence.

Indigo reflects *space* as its essence.

Violet reflects *patience* as its essence.

3. From the beginning we have the promise of the Christ, the sustaining principle of growth and evolution through which we can come to know the ever-presence of God and effect our reunion with Him. Green is the color most appropriately symbolic of growth, evolution (as reflected in the shedding of leaves, the replacement of the old by the new), and the presence of God throughout the natural world. Therefore, its deeper meaning can well be summarized thus: *Green* represents the *Christ Principle.* At this point it might seem that finally we are ready to emerge from our forest. But are we? Vibration, color, the atomic world, spirit, idea, purpose, time, space, patience—all have been related to one another and all have been shown to be represented in the rainbow, the symbol of God's covenant to provide man with the means of salvation. But what of the other forces influencing man in his striving to become reunited with his ultimate source? What of the forces reflected in the heavenly bodies? In the physical body of man himself? As will be seen in the next chapter, these too have a part in the final fulfilling of the covenant, which covers us (as we cover a seed) until we grow into a Tree of Life.

Chapter Five
THE TREE OF LIFE

And he said, Who told thee that thou wast naked?
Hast thou eaten of the tree, whereof I commanded
thee that thou shouldest not eat? Genesis 3:11

And the Lord God said, Behold, the man is become
as one of us, to know good and evil: and now, lest
he put forth his hand, and take also of the tree
of life, and eat, and live forever . . . Genesis 3:22

Let us pause for a moment to review what we have found so far
in our study of vibration, which we discovered to be color. From
color we took off into the earth in search of the smallest root we
could find, and we found an atom, the smallest piece of a root, as a
point of beginning. Here we discovered that the three primary
colors in the pigments are merely shadows of something else—
spirit, idea and purpose—which in turn are but the projections of
the Father, Son and Holy Spirit. To establish a point of reference
we noted that these trinities are reflected in the triangle, which,
since we can think in terms of three dimensions only, is the basic
building block of all matter.

We then moved on to time, space and patience, which we
identified as those tools by which we comprehend our
relationships to the world; and we found that we may be aware of
these tools as color. Also, as we searched among those roots, we
found that forces other than the elemental ones are flowing in the
material world, like the sap of a tree, and coming into
manifestation as various things.

Are we ready to emulate God and project ourselves into a

materialization? Can we, as man, reach for and gain an understanding of God's creation? Can man, who arose from the earth and to the earth must return, reach out to the heavens and pull unto himself, so to speak, that which will allow him to live forever? He knows good and evil—he has eaten of that tree—but can he also know life? Did we or did we not find a bridge between the material world and God, a bridge that has been there all along—the covenant *between* man and his Creator, embodied in the rainbow? If we did, the old saying that there is a pot of gold at the end of the rainbow may yet prove to be more truth than poetry.

The Importance of the Physical Body

In our attempt to discover a connection between ourselves and our Maker, must we always deal in shadows? Must we not, in our seemingly outward reaching toward God, actually reach into ourselves? Do not the colors in the rainbow show that the purpose is to reach toward the center, that the progress is from spirit to idea to purpose and that the arrow of direction—the higher vibrations—always points toward the center of the circle, us? Yet, if we must deal with shadows, let us move from the roots up to the trunk of the tree and see what we can learn of it. (How earthy can we be—we, who call our own torso a trunk?)

We might be at a loss as to how to get to that tree we are trying to find if it were not for Edgar Cayce. Almost two-thirds of his readings were of a physical nature. Some have wondered why he insisted on giving so many readings for sick people rather than discoursing on some other subjects of a more general interest. Yet a close look at the content of those readings reveals a tendency to doctor the soul as much as the physical body.

Was Edgar Cayce trying to tell us something by his interest in the physical body, something beyond the fact that helping some particular person get well was worthwhile? It has been said that Jesus healed the sick and that Edgar Cayce was merely emulating Jesus. This statement could be true, but a natural question seems to follow from it: Why did Jesus put such emphasis on healing? It is true that He said the Kingdom of Heaven is within and the body is the real Temple of God. These things in themselves might be enough to justify the importance both Jesus and Cayce gave to healing. Yet were not they both trying to tell us something more by their healing ministry, something that the people in Jesus' day could not understand and—although Cayce gave us a clue—the people of today (and even now only a few) are just beginning to comprehend?

In many of his physical readings, Cayce made reference to the endocrine system. At the time he gave these readings this system was only beginning to be understood; even today we are many years away from a thorough knowledge of it. In practically every life reading, he referred to the planetary influences that affected the people for whom the reading was given. In both the physical and the life readings the emphasis seems to have been on how the body was influenced by certain forces, whether those deliberately applied or the natural planetary influences.

The life readings pointed to traits of character, habits, skills and other factors developed in previous lives which were a part of the present experience. These carry-overs, called karma (good or bad), affected the body and its reaction to its present life experiences in one way or another; an awareness of such influences could help the individual in its present development along its soul journey. It seems that the physical readings were given for a similar purpose, for often Cayce emphasized the need to change the attitudes, control the emotions and in other ways become a more congenial and useful person—or else, as he sometimes asked, "Why get well?"

Because he related physical well-being to spiritual factors, Edgar Cayce has been said to have tinged his readings with religiosity, which supposedly arose from his being an ardent student of the Bible; but could the true reason that he so consistently linked the physical and the soul have been to point up the essence of another series of readings he gave, a series that in itself is not yet well understood—the readings on the Revelation?

Could it be that both Edgar Cayce and Jesus were trying to tell us that by maintaining a well body we could come to know it as the Temple of God; that in the body we would find the keys to our heaven or our hell, and eventually to our companionship—our oneness, if you please—with God Himself? (How else can we account for Jesus' statement that "Heaven and earth shall pass away, but my words shall not pass away"? [Matt. 24:35] What did He mean by this statement, when all our efforts are to get to heaven so that we can live happily ever after?) Could it be?

That this may be a reason for the emphasis on physical healing is attested to in Cayce's readings, as will be shown. For this study points up *a* way to know ourselves, one that we may not have observed before—a way that opens up to us through the study of vibration as it is portrayed in the readings on the Revelation. When Cayce was asked by a group studying healing and prayer to explain "the general plan and theme, the significance of . . . and give such explanations of the symbols used as will make this book [the Revelation] of personal value to those present seeking to awaken and develop the inner life," the answer was, in part, as follows (see Appendix for entire reading):

Why, then, ye ask now, was this written (this vision) in such a manner that is hard to be interpreted, *save in the experience* of every soul who seeks to know, to walk in, a closer communion with Him? [Author's italics]   281-16

Would not this answer present the reason that the Revelation has been so misunderstood—or noncomprehended? It must be experienced!

The present treatise is not a study of the book of the Revelation; we are concerned with only a part of this book of the Bible, that part which applies directly to our study of vibration.[25] Yet the following passage from the first reading in the Revelation series seems to get to the heart of our study:

For the visions, the experiences, the names, the churches, the places, the dragons, the cities, all are but emblems of *those forces that may war within the individual* in its journey through the material, or from the *entering into the material* manifestation to the entering into the glory, or the *awakening in the spirit,* in the *interbetween, in the borderland, in the shadow.*

Hence we find, as the churches are named, they are as the *forces* that are *known as the senses,* that *must be spiritualized by the will of the individual* made one in the very activities in a material world.

And the elders and the Lamb are the emblems, *are the shadows of those acceptances or rejections that are made in the experiences* of the individual. [Author's italics]   281-16

[25]For a comprehensive study of the Revelation and Edgar Cayce's readings about it, see *A Commentary on the Book of the Revelation,* published by the A.R.E. Press #215P, $5.95

Here we are confronted with two fundamental postulates. First, that all things that we perceive are but *forces* manifesting, that which we see (Hebrews, chapters 8-10) being only shadows of the real; and second, that all experiences are merely a correlation of truths presented, the results of our acceptances and rejections of these truths. Thus the manifested world is but a shadow of the real, and we choose our responses, which cause our experiences— our wars within ourselves (our illnesses). As will be seen, we do all this by way of the colors, which in turn are but shadows. Consider the following:

In seeking, then, do individuals find from the beginning that there is presented, in every line, in every form, that good and bad (as termed) that arises from their activity, in what they do about that knowledge they have respecting the law, the love, the mercy, the understanding of the wherefore of the Lamb's advent into the world . . .   281-16

The above passages seem to be saying that we, in our experiences, are really dealing with the need to know the law regarding the *why* of Jesus (which is a tall order!) Could not this need be enough to justify both Jesus' and Cayce's preoccupation with healing? It is not enough to say that we need a well body; we need to know what goes on in the body so that we can direct our attention inward instead of outward. For the great study for man seems to be aimed toward the knowing of self.

The Endocrine System
and Its Relation to Perception and Response

Besides giving answers to questions about specific portions of the Revelation, these readings seem to be saying, among other things, that the planetary forces (which are the creative forces in man's nature) and the ancient elements of earth, water, fire and air are all sensed by us as colors by way of the endocrine system. The endocrine system then acts through the various centers for recognition of the forces that reach us through our five senses and correlates that perceived with that which we already know—our previous experiences. A point to remember is that we habitually associate our external circumstances with our internal memories and react to them on that basis, rather than relating those

74

happenings to the laws they are meant to reveal to us. When we consider that we are really sensing creative forces, as influences, which present laws, as colors, then we might pay attention to the laws rather than to the memories of previous experiences, which the colors first bring to mind. This process of perception and reaction is outlined in the chart below.

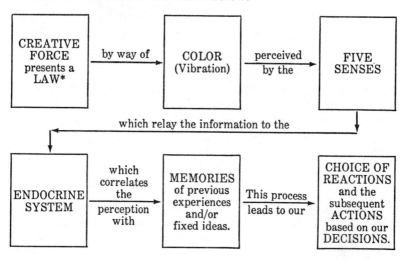

*This is the function of all internal and external stimuli that we receive.

The following excerpt indicates how the forces and our perception of them can influence our development:

... as you each become conscious in your own experience of the movement *of* the influences *through* the body upon the various stages of awareness, there comes a determination, a desire, a longing for the greater light.   281-28

This concept is related to the following passage, given in answer to a question about the horses in the Revelation:

For a reference to these, let each in your study of these, as in relation to the centers themselves, consider the effect of the color itself upon thine own body as ye attempt to apply same by either concentration, dedication or meditating upon these. For as has been given, color is but vibration. Vibration is movement. Movement is activity of a positive and negative force.   281-29

Concerning the planetary forces and their relative colors, we find:

These vary, to be sure, according to the variation of an *experience*. For these are the variable forces in the very nature of man himself, for he partakes of all and from all the influences and forces.281-29

Careful reading of the above (together with the other passages on the Revelation included herein) may lead us to realize that the forces (idea, spirit and purpose) in the vibrations that reach us via our five senses stimulate us to respond according to our memory of how we have used these forces before. But in responding in this way we are taking our memories, which are but *shadows* of the laws, as a predicate for our reactions; and is not the *spirit*-part of the vibration that to which we are meant to respond—in spirit? What did Cayce say about this? In a passage on the purpose of the Revelation we find:

Rather was it not to present it that each entity, each soul, might find within itself *that which answers to that within,* that makes the real answer to that as was before stated, "My Spirit beareth witness with thy spirit"? 281-31

Then our growth (or our failure to grow) depends upon our responses one to another; for do we not respond in kind—our spirit to the spirit of others, our ideas to their ideas, our purposes to their purposes? Color tone to color tone, we receive stimuli from and return them to each other.

In order that we may see how these colors (that is, the creative forces that are already in us) work, let us now examine in more detail the various forces in the colors, together with some of their relationships. Here we may find those "patterns of response" (the "leaves of the trees [which] are for the healing of the nations," 281-16) that can determine the growth of our tree. For remember what Cayce said:

Know first that the knowledge of God is a growing thing, for ye grow in grace, in knowledge, in understanding *as* ye apply that ye KNOW. But remember, as has been given by Him, to know to do good and do it not is sin. 281-30

Let us start from the outside color in the rainbow and move inward, even as we receive outside stimuli through our five senses and use them to attain an inner knowledge of their purpose. Part of our aim will be to correlate the colors of the rainbow with the energy centers—that is, the members of the endocrine system—within the body. Further, since man is a replica of the universe, we shall correlate these planetary forces within the body with the planetary forces of the solar system.

The following chart summarizes the relationships we will be investigating in this section and correlates this material with that which was covered in the preceding chapter. Though for the sake of clarity we will be considering each glandular center separately, we should remember that one center cannot act independently of the other glands, for the endocrine system acts as a *system*, not as separate glandular operations. (See chart.)

The First Center

The gonad center is the seat from which we respond to fleshly needs, for Saturn, the planetary correlate of the gonads, is the influence operating here. It is the seat of propagation—not just procreation, but the propagation of our desires, our habits, the spirit we would show to others; it is the center of that which must be tested in response from others, for Saturn is the influence that is "the beginning of earthly woes, that to which all insufficient matter is cast for the beginning." (900-10)

Pure creative energy enters the body here, according to Cayce, and thus we color our responses to one another on the basis of the *controlling factors* in our memory that have been stimulated. If our choice of response is insufficient to express adequately our need or understanding, this remolding force acts to help us with a next or subsequent choice which may be in a similar vein. Should our response be contrary to what we know to do, then Saturn acts to bring to us, by attraction from others, our karma, or it acts to correct our insufficiencies. Or if our responses are those arising only from imbalanced habits, the creative force moves through the body in such a fashion as to abuse or neglect some bodily function, causing us to get sick. Then Saturn must act to cure the imbalance, again bringing about the remolding of our insufficient reactions.

COLORS	MATERIAL WORLD Atomic Manifestation Vibrations	MENTAL WORLD Activating Principles	Consciousness-Evolving Principles	SPIRITUAL WORLD (symbolized in Rainbow) Material Symbols (Planets)	Spiritual (Creative-Motivative) Forces	Man's Awareness	ENDOCRINE SYSTEM	LORD'S PRAYER Crucifixion of Self	SAVIOR Covenant
Violet		Patience →	Patience	Jupiter	Strength	Understanding (Acceptance)	Pituitary	Heaven	
Indigo		Space		Mercury	Mind	Relationships	Pineal	Name	
Blue	Purpose			Uranus	Psychic	Ideals (Purpose)	Thyroid	Will	
Green			Self (Ego)	Venus	Love	Changes (Growth, Love)	Thymus	Evil	Christ Principle
Yellow	Idea			Mars	Madness	Reactions (Karma)	Solar Plexus	Debts	
Orange		Time		Neptune	Mystic	Choices	Lyden	Temptation	
Red	Spirit (Energy)			Saturn	Beginning	Desires	Gonad	Bread	

It can readily be seen why we need so many shades of red; as Edgar Cayce said:

> ... while red is anger, rosy to most souls means delight and joy—yet to others, as they are formed in their transmission from center to center, come to mean or to express what *manner* of joy; whether that as would arise from a material, a mental or a spiritual experience. 281-30

The Second Center

Next in our scale is the lyden center (cells of Leydig), which is correlated with that influence which Cayce says is "that of Neptune as of mystic" (900-10) and with the color orange, which we have related to the mystery of time. While we comprehend time by reason of orange, there is another force operating here, one that pertains to our choices. This is the seat of choices, as stressed in the command "I have set before you life and death ... choose life." (Deut. 30:19) Thus it relates to temptation. It is here that we give life to our choices, our habits, those memories that form a pattern of response which we allow to control our reactions. Certainly from here come the choices which must eventually be "weighed in the balance," not just the decisions between good and evil, but those that reflect the measure of our understanding of the choice in all its relationships, for the lyden gland has been called by Cayce the seat of the soul in the body.

This activity of the lyden gland, or the force of Neptune, relating as it does to time and the weighing of ideas, is also related to life itself in a fascinating way which points up the "mystic" faculties Edgar Cayce mentions:

> Is the First Cause, then, that the separation of God in the desire for companionship with Himself, that as created or brought into a material manifestation the reverse of love, of hope, of patience, of all the attributes that are the spirit of activity, the *moving influence* or force?
>
> This we see manifested in a physical body through the glandular system—as the activity of conception, the *dividing* of the activity of the gland itself, that brings conception.
>
> Thus, this is the first of the centers from which arises all that is movement, to bring into being both the face and the preface—or the

back, or the reverse—in the experience.[26] [Author's italics]281-51

Neptune, the force which spawned the life in the sea that evolved into man and which has existed from the beginning of God's desire for companionship, certainly must be one of the cardinal forces in us. Is it any wonder we are so involved with time (it is life itself)? It is the correlating force between spirit (red) and idea (yellow) by which we measure our worth to God, are weighed in the balance—and are found wanting until we eventually become *equal* with our Creator. Orange is a beautiful color, and we need to respect the rider of the horse with the scales. (Rev., chapter 4)

The Third Center

The solar plexus center (the readings indicate this phrase is preferable to *adrenal center*, though the center does include the adrenal glands) is correlated with the planet Mars and has been called the storehouse of karma. Certainly it is the source of our fears; but it is also the source of our strengths, for does not the "fight or flight" of the adrenalin reaction make us either rulers of the beast-man or cowards before him? The lion is a tawny yellow beast, and the coward is called yellow; both strike their colors to the music of our debts or draw the ire and fire of our enemies.

Edgar Cayce says that the force of Mars is that of madness, which is somewhat different from the force generally attributed to this planet. Consider, though, the unreasonableness of holding grudges; of holding too long to ideas that need to be changed, thus making a single mistake over and over again; of holding an attachment for things, which are but manifested ideas; or of knowing what we ought to do and not doing it. Is it not madness to act in these ways? Is it not also madness to want to avoid paying our debts to one another, for did not Jesus say that "every jot and

---

[26]Perhaps Goethe's arranging of colors in a circle could be associated with the lemniscate (see pg. 88) and with the simultaneous origin of both sides of anything (referred to here as "the face and the preface ... the back, or the reverse . . ."). If, as he suggested, the perception of any color brings about a physiological need to see its opposite, the color wheel could also indicate our need to see, or be aware of, the Law of Opposites. Goethe's color wheel contained only six colors.

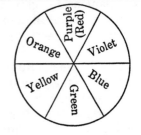

tittle" (Matt. 5:18) must be paid? Is it not madness to disbelieve or to act like we do not know the truth of the law "Whatsoever a man soweth, that shall he also reap"? (Gal. 6:7)

Yes, Mars relates to debts, to the madness that man expressed in choosing to use his own will, in choosing to act so as to rebel against and forget his Maker. Thus is it any wonder that Mars, as that force in man *before* he came into the earth plane, is still active in the ideas expressed by man himself through his actions? Yes, Mars is the force of action—but that action can be directed toward paying the debt man owes to his Maker and even to himself. All the possible weaknesses and strengths that can arise from the use of this force are based on an *idea* being the predicate for reaction, and *yellow* is the color that triggers in man the ideas that rule him. The adrenal glands, in fact, happen to be yellow, further underlining the previously delineated relationship between this color and ideas.

The Fourth Center

The fourth center, the thymus or heart center, is correlated with Venus, aptly called the goddess of love, and it must have its place in man, or how could he recognize it? The thymus gland is the seat of that force we call love; it is the seat, too, of the personality, for do we not point to the area of the heart when we refer to ourselves? Who has not known the aching heart in sorrow? Must not we have a point within us that we can call the center of our cares? We say that we have thoughts in our head, but who has not said, "In my heart I know"?

Where, then, is the seat of the self? Not in the heart, but near it, in that gland known as the thymus, or the seat of evil. Has not Cayce said that the only sin is that of self—selfishness? Is it not from here that we love—a person or a thing—and hurt when we lose either? Is it not the force of love that changes our dislike for someone into concern for him? Is it not the force of love that changes a bad man into a good one? Is it not love that sustains us throughout life as we lose the things we like and learn to live with those we do not like—sometimes even to love them? Is not the seat of the personality involved when we change our minds, especially in regard to something about which we have felt strongly? Would not this change be similar to the one evidenced by the green in the forest—our likes withering and dying, later growing again in some other direction, just as new leaves replace the old?

Would not green be the symbol which would portray these activities best? Do we not see as green jealousy and envy, yet also love, the healing force which changes it all? Do we not gratify our appetites through indulging our wants until we must change? Green is certainly the color of change, as it is of growth and decay. But this is that same force which will allow us to take the wings of the eagle and fly, not only above our troubles and earthly desires, but even to other realms of consciousness.[27] Does not the appearance and disappearance of green in the earth symbolize to us obedience to the cyclic laws of nature? Is not this force, then— which we perceive through the color green—clearly representative of the Christ Principle, which is love?

The Fifth Center

We now move from the centers which are heavily tinged with the earthly forces, such as procreation, gratification, sustenance and preservation, to those associated with forces of a mental and spiritual import, which concern the reason for man's being in the earth. The first of these higher centers is the thyroid, related to the force that man calls will and associated with the planet Uranus. It is hard for us to grasp the significance of this unless we look at how Cayce described this planet's influence. He said, "In that of Uranus as of the psychic," (900-10) and, "In Uranus we find the extremes, and the interest in the occult—or the mystical." (2571-1)

In many references to Uranus, Cayce placed heavy emphasis on the force of extremes and an interest in the mystical, but let us consider some of will's aspects from an everyday standpoint, that of the ongoing battle most of us have with our will. We are continually faced with choices of reactions of one kind or another. Some of these reactions we hold on to almost mystically (that is, for reasons so much beyond our understanding that we would have trouble explaining them in down-to-earth terms). Some we let go of rather easily. Not all the ways we act or react are as matters of life or death to us, but the relativity of extremes can easily be seen. As to our will itself, why do we all cherish our free will so much if it is not a mystical thing? Is it not this very will

---

[27]Was it by chance only that the first craft to land on the moon— symbolically, at least, another plane of consciousness—was named the "Eagle"?

that at times gives us the drive to overcome seemingly insurmountable odds? Can one deny that the force which causes one person to bow to the will of another, especially when two strong-willed people meet, is a psychic one?

Considering these aspects of the will says nothing, however, about its proper role as expressed in the Lord's Prayer: "Thy will be done in earth as it is in heaven." We repeat this prayer very frequently, sometimes daily, but how often do we actually set our will aside so that we can see what would happen? We resist what we do not like with all our might, never remembering the prayer—the promise—to allow God to have His way with us. Yet, for some, when we really do stand aside and allow God to take over, are there not literally miracles? Miracles we can hardly believe! But to do this is not easy until one learns how, and even then it is seldom that we want to follow this course.

In our study we have said that blue relates to purpose. Where is there purpose in letting go of our will and allowing God's will to be done? But who said anything about letting go of our will? The strongest use of will there is, is to be found in holding our will in check while God's will is done in us. *That* is the whole purpose of man's involvement in the earth plane—to learn to return to God that which was freely given in the first place. Since God gave us free will—of His own free choice—how can we ever be equal with, God unless we also give our free will? We must emulate God before we can be His companions!

Since, according to Edgar Cayce, "Psychic is of the soul," (5752-5) to make full use of this force we must hold the conscious mind, our ego, in check and allow the mind of the soul to direct our reactions; and thus we bring the universal consciousness into materiality. Only in this way can we, like Jesus, become an atom, a pure unit of being, in the consciousness of God. In doing this we literally "live by faith," becoming our purpose and expressing that part of the whole we are to become. The blue (purpose) in the atom, which is the same as that in the rainbow, fulfills the promise of the Savior expressed in the green. It is certainly most fitting that green is the color just below blue in the rainbow, for Christ is the servant of all.

The Sixth Center

The sixth center, the second of the higher centers, is the pineal, related to the planet Mercury, which pertains to mind. If we were content to act on the phrase "Let this mind be in you, which was also in Christ Jesus," (Phil. 2:5) all might be well. Yet would we be satisfied to do so? Is it not by using the mind that we separate concepts, name them, compare one with another, make choices or responses, and decide which of them we like and which we dislike? Can we find even one person who would choose not to use his mind? But just how much do we know about mind? It seems that we usually think of mind as a function rather than a force in itself, for we rate intelligence by I.Q. tests and place great value on instant recall. Psychiatry attributes a great deal of importance to the operation of the mind, but all the while it asks, "What is mind?"

It seems that science is just beginning to discover the many bodily functions related to the pineal gland. An early concept regarding the pineal was that it was perhaps a third eye, though atrophied. Later thinking regarded it as a portion of the body that, through the process of evolution, has become unnecessary in man's present state. Yet if Cayce was right, the pineal in conjunction with the lyden has more to do with the soul function of man than any other portion of the body, an importance that is reflected even in the physical development of the human embryo: "The cord that is eventually known or classified as the pineal is the first movement that takes place of a physical nature through the act of conception . . ." (281-46)

Of the Mercurian influence itself, Cayce said, "As in Mercury pertaining of mind." (900-10) And of mind he said, "Mind being that control of, or being the spark of the Maker, the *will*, the individual when we reach the plane of man." (3744-1) Thus, if nothing more, the force of Mercury is that power which keeps us individually oriented. Who among us would trade personalities with another so as to *be* him? None, for we all want very much to be ourselves.

Throughout the Cayce readings there is an insistence that "Mind is the builder." Mind, then, is that factor which recognizes our separation from others; hence it is the cognizing force that pertains to knowing itself, for the knowing of *anything* is a factor of, or pertains to, the operation of mind. Mind is certainly that which allows us to distinguish relationships between all things. Since we are in an active, changing world, mind must certainly be related to space itself, for it is mind that measures these changing relationships (that is, brings us to some *understanding of relationships*) and causes us to decide how we are to react to them.

Once we have decided anything, the force of mind, or Mercury, executes that decision *automatically*. Hence the only power man has, really, is the power of choice! The activity through the body is determined by preconditioning and is a result of that first injunction, "I have set before you life and death ... choose life ..." (Deut. 30:19) But what causes the preconditioning? Edgar Cayce said that it was caused by *us* as we *name* those forces, ideas or concepts which we allow to rule us.

Consider the following answer, which he gave when asked if the pineal were related to the upheavals mentioned in the sixth chapter of the Revelation:

Correct, but this would have to be *relatively* so. For these are at those periods when, in the colors that these arise to—which are of the purple, they become rather such that there *must* be the *disseminating* or the giving away of the egoism of self. 281-29

And again, when asked whether the pineal is to be associated with the word *name* in the Lord's Prayer, Cayce said, "Relatively, yes." (281-29) This "relatively" was pursued further in the next reading:

There is a Name to each soul. For He hath called His own *by name!* What name? All the names that may have been as a material experience through an earthly sojourn, or all the names that may have been through the experience of an entity in that environ or those relative associations of Venus, Mars, Jupiter, Uranus, Saturn, Sun, Moon, or what! Or a Name that is above *every* name!
. . . every influence—you see—is *relative!* Hence the name is relative to that which is accomplished by the soul in its sojourn throughout its whole experience . . . 281-30

It may readily be seen that here Cayce has given a basis for understanding the mind's reactions to what the soul has done throughout its evolution. Mind, or the force of Mercury, may seem to *force* a reaction which is relative to the accomplishments of the soul that have preceded any decision. Since the sum total of all experience is not known by the conscious mind but is known by the subconscious,[28] it makes sense that some of our choices of action bring unexpected and sometimes unwanted results. These results we call karma—and we generally resist them, for they are not what we expected; when the results are harmonious with our wishes, we call them good because we like them. The idea, though, is really not whether the results are "good" or "bad," or whether we like them or not; it is simply that mind is the builder and no stone (no force or concept we have named) can be left out of the structure we are building! And we are building physical, mental and spiritual bodies by what we do in the physical, for:

Hence we find that the mental body is both finite and infinite—a part of self and yet a part of a universal consciousness—or the mind of the Maker.   1650-1

Consider the "giving away of egoism," mentioned in 281-29 above, in conjunction with the functions of the mind, which must correlate the desired result with all past experiences. Would not the ego do better to give away its claim to that desire rather than have to accept what it did not want? Undoubtedly it would. But how can this be done when our desire for what we want is so strong?

The answer is found in the Lord's Prayer (in the phrase "Thy will be done," taken together with, "Lead us not into temptation"). Exploring such answers is outside the range of our study of vibration. These ideas have been touched upon in this treatise because the study of the forces moving through the body, as colors, is necessary for us to gain a concept of the complexity of our subject. And yet, there is also a simplicity to vibration, which must become obvious as we trace our roots back to the Savior of man, promised in the rainbow.

The Seventh Center

"Our Father, which art in heaven" relates to our call upon the forces of Jupiter, represented in the body as the pituitary and

---

[28]That the conscious mind cannot know enough to make the proper correlations is shown by the black (that is, unknown) horse in the Revelation. This symbol represents the unconscious forces brought into action by conscious choices made in the mind and activated in the body at the lyden level.

related to violet—the softest of colors, yet that of the greatest strength, for Edgar Cayce characterized these forces thus: "In Jupiter as strength." (900-10) The strength is that which allows us to endure all things until we finally attain understanding. It certainly is the endurance factor in our lives, and we generally relate the word patience to endurance. We have associated patience with the color violet, and the Cayce readings support the relationship between this color and Jupiter. Scientifically, the pituitary is the master gland of the body, controlling all bodily functions; thus it is a source of strength to the entire being. Cayce says the same thing, and much more, in the following:

> In Jupiter we find the great ennobling influences, the broad-mindedness, the ability to consider others, the universal consciousnesses that are a part of the entity's unfoldment.
>
> 2890-2

Is this master gland important in mental and spiritual as well as physical activity? It seems that the pituitary takes the choices made by the mind and activates the rest of the body to carry out whatever decisions are made; thus it operates at all levels of decision and brings the choices into manifestation at the physical level.

The following passages describe what may be the greatest function of the pituitary:

> Patience is the lesson that each soul must learn in its sojourn through materiality.
>
> And in patience then does man become more and more aware *of* the continuity of life, of his soul being a portion of the Whole; patience being the portion of man's sphere of activity in the finite being, as time and space manifest the creative and motivative forces.
>
> 1554-3

Does not this reading point to the highest purpose of man's being, the very reason for his existence in the earth? Would not this conclusion be especially appropriate if the pituitary does indeed relate to patience, which we sense as violet? It seems that the question is very much like the color—delicate, yet the most important, for without it the rest would be meaningless.

In view of its total functioning, can the endocrine system be called the Tree of Life? The answer may well be both yes and no, for before we reach a definite conclusion we need to see if such an identification is consistent with the admonition that "of the tree of the knowledge of good and evil [life] thou shalt not eat..." (Gen. 2:17)

Edgar Cayce has indicated that creative energy enters the body at the gonad level, from where, as a result of our choices, it moves through the body to carry out, to manifest, these choices of action. This does seem to be what happens in everyday living. When a vibration reaches us through our five senses, the bodily forces, moving in the form of the lemniscate,[29] carry it throughout the body, where the endocrine centers separate the vibration into its various components of spirit, idea and purpose.[30] The various endocrine centers, acting somewhat as a sieve, then send their analysis along the "silver cord" back to the brain as color, the color of the ideas, spirit and purposes included in the vibration. The brain, in turn, associates these components, via memory, with an experience of one kind or another by the use of color tones, which can be considered harmonious or inharmonious. The mind then chooses a response according to whether it likes or dislikes the *experience* associated with the color and whether it understands or fails to understand that experience. This choice is carried to the pituitary gland, which through nerve channels activates the body to respond according to that particular choice of reaction (which, incidentally, shows through the aura also).

This choice, along with other similar ones, gradually causes us to react similarly to the remembered experiences, so that there comes into being a *pattern* of response which may be expected from us whenever a certain memory is recalled. Thus our typical reactions become routine and, like the leaves upon our tree, develop into the patterns of expressions of purpose, ideals, prejudices, habits, and abilities by which others recognize us.

---

[29]The term lemniscate refers to the figure ∞. The bodily forces move vertically in a figure-eight pattern through the body.

[30]In order to facilitate our presentation, we are using only one vibration for our illustration. Actually, many vibrations reach us at all times, and the process described here merely illustrates what is happening to a single one.

At the point of choice, or because of it, we come to *expect* a result, and, in dealing with one another, we hold this expectancy until there is a response. If perchance the response is not what was expected, we not only are disarmed, but must make another choice, which may or may not stimulate the desired response. In relation to the physical body, if this expectancy is not awakened the results are disastrous. Consider the following:

... the expectancy of the physical body must be awakened before the body, through its tissue, its vital forces, can emanate the necessary building, or eliminating forces, of the physical body, to rebuild or develop properly. Hence the cause of death in [the] physical world.   900-21

Most of us live by habit patterns to such an extent that we are described in terms of them. These patterns are like the leaves on our personality tree, and they must be changed or they would live on forever, making it impossible for us to grow through the development of new patterns of expression. Death in the physical and consequent reincarnation, then, are necessary so that we may change our expressions, our leaves. Edgar Cayce said it was not necessary that we change, but it was by the grace of God that we do!

On the surface, this analogy of the Tree of Life seems like a very good one. The operation outlined above, through millions of responses, life after life, surely will get us back to the Father, will it not? Would we not after lifetimes and lifetimes be able to live as we should? Maybe. We must, however, consider free will, through which we make our choices. Note carefully all of reading 900-21, presented in the Appendix, before rejecting or accepting this analogy.

Certainly it is by way of the tree described above and our resultant leaves, as patterns of expression, that we come to know good and evil. The Tree of Good and Evil we eat of—and surely we die! At least the personality does. How, then, can we eat of the Tree of Life and live forever? The answer, again, is quite simple. It is to be found in the Lord's Prayer: "Thy will be done in earth as it is in heaven." In living this prayer we *accept* whatever "bread" is best for us, meet our karma (our debts) in love, and leave the "ability to serve," the glory (262-92), to God. We claim nothing of ourselves, for we are following the example given by Jesus when He said, "I can do nothing of myself; but as my Father hath taught me, I speak these things." (John 8:28) If we lived in this way, how would the operation of the forces within us be different (if it would be different at all) from what it generally is? How would our tree function and develop, and what or who would form the leaves, our expressions?

Up to the point where our reaction is chosen, the forces would operate exactly as we have described; but then, instead of making a choice based on our desires and memories, we would literally "wait on the Lord" (Ps. 27:14) for a choice of response to become evident through the body. To function in this way we still the conscious mind, and the subconscious mind—which knows *all* our experiences[31] and recognizes which bread would best serve (or feed) us—finds via attunement those experiences we need to remember and act upon in order best to serve the god which we worship. This in turn brings the correct reaction—the one most in accord with our purpose and ideals—into the present from whatever life we have experienced it in. Thus there is "called to mind" (John 14:26) all that we have done, even "from the foundations of the world." (Matt. 13:35) We become, literally, universal, because all lives become as one life and we live forever.

The creative forces (the planetary ones) are directed by us as we repeat the Lord's Prayer and demonstrate that we mean it. We lay aside our will and thus allow the remolding of our expressions (our bread), paying those debts we acknowledge (in justice) and asking to be relieved of our choices. This brings about our participation in the greater life as we learn to serve others instead of self. Remember, with this prayer we ourselves direct the creative forces through us according to our memories, experiences and needs. In this way they come to obey us; we become their ruler and thus, eventually, co-creators with God!

In this context, "Wait on the Lord" refers to much more than just daily meditation—it comes to mean meditating before each altar of sacrifice of our will for that of the Father. Every one of our desires must be offered up to the creative forces. It is not up to us to pick and choose which desire is to be offered; rather, the sacrifice is to be made of each as it is aroused by the vibration that

---

[31]Dr. Carl G. Jung has said that modern man does not yet realize that he is entirely dependent on the cooperation of the unconscious.

reaches us. We must meet them in turn by standing still before the Lord. In other words, we must adopt the attitude expressed by Jesus: "... let this cup pass from me: nevertheless not as I will, but as thou wilt." (Matt. 26:39)

As indicated in the following excerpt from the readings, vibration is both the key to achieving this development and the criterion by which our oneness with God can be recognized:

> For, without passing through each and every stage of development, there is not the correct vibration to become one with the Creator, beginning with the first vibration, as is of the spirit quickened with the flesh, and made manifest in material world (earth's plane).   900-16

This passage also provides a concept of why it is necessary to go back to the original creation to get an understanding of a vibration, for it points out that the vibratory patterns established in the very beginning continue on throughout our development in the earth plane.

The same reading also shows how important our fleshly existence is to this process of development (perhaps this importance is one reason for the readings' emphasis on physical healing, which we questioned earlier in this chapter): "... and each stage of development made manifest through flesh, which is the *testing portion of the universal vibration*." [Author's italics] (900-16)

It really is simple. If we accept responsibility for our conscious and unconscious memory patterns (that is, if we learn patience), we find that the Tree of Life is within, and we can eat of that tree only in the Garden of Eden. The Cayce readings indicate that by adopting the pattern given us in the Christ we ourselves can become the Tree of Life:

> For each experience in the earth is as a schooling, is as an experience for the soul. For how gave He? He is the vine and ye are the branches, or He *is* the source and ye are the trees. As the tree falls so does it lie. *There* it begins when it has assimilated, when it has applied in *spiritual* reaction that it has gained.   262-99

Summary

Our study of vibration has taken us back to the initial creation, to the origin of the creative forces in man's nature, the planetary forces that are experienced within us as color. In our investigation of these influences we relied heavily on the Revelation material given in the Cayce readings. Here are some of the main concepts we encountered in our attempt to understand the nature of these forces, how we perceive them, and how we can use them to develop into a Tree of Life:

1. The majority of the Cayce readings deal with physical healing. This could indicate that the key to man's eventual regaining of companionship with his Creator is to be found within the physical body. The frequency with which Cayce referred to the endocrine system led us to concentrate on this system in our effort to comprehend the role of the body in man's spiritual development. The endocrine centers are the focal points of the creative forces that influence man to react in various ways. Our investigation of how they influence our choice of response brought us to the conclusion that we generally react on the basis of our memories of previous experiences, memories that are evoked by the colors via which we perceive these forces; but since our memories are merely shadows, would we not do better to respond to the universal laws which are the essence that the vibrations are presenting to us? This process of perception and response is illustrated in the chart on page 75.

2. The creative planetary forces experienced within the body as vibration correlate well with the external forces of the solar system. A brief description of the activity of each of these forces was given, including the color through which we become aware of it, the specific endocrine center in which its influence is focused, some of the ways in which it can affect us, and how we can use it in our spiritual growth. The relationships we derived in this section of the chapter are shown in the chart on page 78.

3. The vibrations we receive through our five senses are analyzed in the endocrine centers and transmitted as color to the brain, which associates them with previous experiences of one sort or another. These associations form the basis of our choices of response. In this way we build up habitual patterns of expressions which, like the leaves of a tree, enable others to recognize us. But, also like the leaves of a tree, these patterns must be shed and replaced with new ones if we are to grow and develop. The example set by Jesus shows that the way of spiritual

development lies in surrendering our will to the Father's. As we still the conscious mind and "wait on the Lord" to make His will known to us, we avoid basing our decisions upon our own memories and desires, which are but shadows, and we allow the subconscious to bring to mind all that we have ever done. Thus we eat of the Tree of Life, and we become rulers of the creative forces, co-creators with God.

Finally, it seems, we have identified the tree we have been studying throughout this treatise on vibration. Finally we have traced its roots, many of which at first glance can seem quite unrelated, through a veritable maze and have arrived at the Tree of Life. It might appear that our task is now completed, for we have followed the roots of our tree all the way back to its trunk, which we discovered to be located—of all places—within ourselves; but surely there is more to a tree than roots and a trunk. In our final chapter we shall consider some (but by no means all) of the branches—some of the many ramifications of vibration.

Chapter Six
PANDORA'S BOX

We now have time to rest and see where we are. We have located ourselves, and from our point of vantage we can look out over our domain, which, once it and all its ramifications are properly understood, we find is really the world of color. We can, by allowing ourselves to become universal, move from the world of shadows into that of reality, where we become one with the creative forces themselves. We recognize the forces by their colors and by such come to know their essences, leaving the world of shadows and moving into the light of self-understanding. "Know thyself" becomes meaningful now, though only because we have the tools to dig for that pot of gold at the foot of the rainbow and we understand their use. Surely that pot of gold is there, for Edgar Cayce told us of "Gold, that [force that] is a renewal," (281-27) and we can by the colors renew our oneness with the Father.

Time as a measure is a cup that must one day be broken; and space is that cord of relationship between separated man and God which must one day be cut. These, time and space, act as mercies of God that weigh us in the scales of justice; and, as we test the creative forces in the crucible of experience, we weigh our involvements and come to know that in patience we possess our souls.

Our search through the roots in the forest has led us to the Tree of Life, but we find ourselves still boxed into a body, unable to be free of the shackles of time and space and our attendant karma. Some have said we are trapped in the flesh, and truly we are. We are yet involved in the results of our having pushed into the flesh, caught in the folds of karmic ties which relentlessly enfold us as we make our choices of reaction to the events that happen to us. The trouble is that we are not yet willing to surrender our desires. We are yet tempted to try the creative forces and watch for the results. We make our choices and the most surprising things happen—often things we wish to avoid. Thus vibration, because of the frequently unexpected effects that our uses of it can have, is truly a Pandora's box. Cayce gave this explanation of the cause-and-effect aspect of our applications of vibration:

As ye attune thine own mechanical instruments to the vibrations of this or that sending influence, ye receive that which is being sent out or vibrated *upon* that plane.   261-15

One point worth noting before we look at some of the specific uses of vibration is that there is a greater range of vibrations than we are generally aware of physically. Cayce said that there are colors above and below those in the spectrum and that the other planes of consciousness (those we experience between earthly lifetimes) are also composed of matter, but of a higher vibration. In this light, consider the colors sometimes seen in dreams, which consist of such hues and tones that they can be described only as "colors which are out of this world" or "colors more gorgeous than any seen on earth"; yet we recognize them to be the same colors as those we see in day-to-day life. Could this be because they are reflecting to us the same laws as the everyday colors, but are doing so in a way that enables us to perceive these laws more clearly and plainly? Or consider the "music of the spheres." Are there not those who have heard this and can describe it only as music never heard on earth? Are such colors and music not just vibrations of a higher qualitative rate than those of which the conscious mind is normally aware?

Telepathy

Now let us examine some of the phenomena that we discover when we open the Pandora's box of vibration. One which intrigues most of us is telepathy (as well as clairvoyance and clairaudience).

We use vibration perceived through all our senses to arrive at a *composite* of vibration. This in turn, because of memory, gives us an awareness of our identity in a certain time and place, as well as mental concepts whereby we relate to what we see and do. This gives rise to a natural question: Would it be possible, through imagination and the stilling of the activity of our five senses, to be aware of what may be happening in some other time or place?

A simple way to test this is to close one's eyes, still the five senses (as in meditation), and try to remember exactly what was happening twenty-four hours previously. The trick is to try to remember the vibratory composite rather than the stimulus that brought our awareness. Ordinarily we remember the stimulus which evoked our reaction at that time and place rather than the total composite, and thus we fail to re-experience fully the events of the day before.

This brings up three points we should note. The first is that by this experiment we readily see that most of us cannot deliberately experience telepathy, for if we could remember the vibratory composite from yesterday, it would cause us to locate ourselves then and there—and we would actually *be* in yesterday. In like manner, could we not go back a week, a month, a year, or clear back to our birth? Is it possible to do this? Edgar Cayce said that it is; in fact, he said that it was through attunement to whatever was being sought that he gave all his readings. He said, too, that all of us have the ability to do this, if we would but pay the price.

The second point to consider is that though the attunement is an activity of the subconscious mind, it is merely subliminal. We can be aware of the colors in various vibratory composites if we try, and thus we can attune ourselves to any place and any time. But it is most difficult to do this, for, by training and habit, we tend to pay attention to the memories aroused by the vibration received by the five senses, and it is natural that we do so.

The third point to consider is that our subconscious minds are more universal in nature than our conscious minds, and thus they are attuned to much more than normally reaches awareness. When we accidentally still our five senses, we have not necessarily stilled the mind. It may well be that at these times we are aware of other composites of vibration, ones that are seemingly not related to those which had just been occupying our conscious mind; when this happens, we momentarily become aware of strange happenings—strange because for a while we find ourselves located somewhere else, and we know an experience called telepathy. If the attunement were to an experience that had not yet happened, but which we find out did happen later on, we would call it precognition. The variations on what we can become aware of in this way are limited only by our imagination; but this does in fact limit them, for it could well be that we get glimpses of the past and future which are of such a nature that we try *not* to be aware of them. We then deliberately stop what we call our psychic ability.

But what are some of the other phenomena that can be accounted for by the mind's ability to tune in to what we might term other realms of consciousness? One may well be the apparent telepathy between humans and plants that has been so well attested to by Cleve Baxter. We have postulated that "mind" is a part of each and every atom, as well as a part of life itself. Is there any logical reason to presume that the *life* in a plant is a different life from ours? Is not all life one life—just manifesting in different forms?

Another ability of ours that can be realized through this attunement process is communication with those who have passed into another dimension or consciousness through the transition called death. Cayce explained this ability as follows:

Each and every soul entity, or earthly entity, passing through the earth's plane, radiates in that plane those conditions that are radiated from the soul or spiritual entity in the individual... When this body, Edgar Cayce, is in the psychic or subconscious condition, he is able then to reach all the subconscious minds, when directed to such subconscious minds by suggestion, whether in the material world or in the spiritual world...   900-22

But is it possible for the rest of us (not just Edgar Cayce) to so communicate with those who have passed on? In sleep, yes:

... we have as the illustration of this condition in the body [900]. We have when this entity enters the subconsciousness, through the medium of laying aside the conscious mind, the projection of the spiritual guide, the father, the thoughts, the impressions, as would be given by that entity, entering the subconsciousness of [900].
   Q-4. Are those radiations like a vibratory force on our earth's plane, such as light wave?
   A-4. May be compared to same, but of the spiritual radiation, and not material radiation; that is, those radiations as come from spirit

may take form in vibratory radiation of color, or light, through the individual's attunement. 900-22

Here again, Cayce answers more than just the original question. He emphasizes the difference between material and spiritual vibration, yet he affirms that both take form in color. This implies that we have a need to comprehend those vibratory forces above and below the known vibratory scale. If we do have such a need, there is reason to believe that we are subliminally aware of much, much more than we think we are. One example of this type of perception would be the subliminal awareness of the aura of another person.

Consider also the following information about attunement with those who have passed on:

Q-1. Is it possible for those that have passed into the spirit plane to at all times communicate with those in the earth plane?

A-1. Yes and no—for these conditions are as has been described— that the *necessary* way or mode must be prepared; for as this: Ever has that vibration as is attracted and thrown off been active in the world as is exercised through that called the telephone, but without proper connection, without shorts, without any disturbance, may proper communication be made? These have not always been active to the *physical* body ... Just the same in that pattern. Those in the astral plane are not always ready. Those in the physical plane are not always ready. What conditions arise (is asked) that we in the physical plane are not ready? ... There are those same elements as has been outlined, of that of the development going on, and the willingness of that *individual* to communicate, as given, see? but when set aright, these may—until passed into that Oneness, or returned again, or gone on beyond such communications. . .

Q-5. Is the effort for spirit communication as much effort on the part of the spirit entity as the effort that should be made on the part of the material or physical entity?

A-5. The force should never be applied, and may never be applied and be real, in either case. The willingness and the desire from both is necessary for the perfect communication, see? Illustrate this same condition by that physical condition as is seen in attunement of either that called radio, or of that called phone, or that of any of that vibratory force as is set by the electron in the material plane. Necessary for the perfect union that each be in accord. In other words, we find many in the astral plane *seeking* to give force active in the material. Many in the material *seeking* to delve into the astral. They must be made one, would they bring the better.   5756-4

As this passage indicates, the radio provides the simplest illustration that what we receive depends on what we are attuned to. And do we not each attune our minds and hearts to our desires? Why, then, do we frequently find that what we attract to ourselves is not wholly to our liking? Surely that which we receive is determined by what we want; but if what we want is not in accord with what we need for our spiritual development, there is a good chance that we will not like the results at all. In relation to this, consider Cayce's answer to the question "How can I best draw people of the right vibration to me?"

By the correct vibration in self. Like begets like. Toned to a tone brings the proper tone from the perfect radiation of such. Each entity *radiates* that tone, that reflection of the concept of its creative force. Each entity—each atom of the entity radiates that vibration to which it attunes itself. Each entity contacts, each entity brings that about itself by putting into action laws, those conditions, those individuals, those vibrations that are necessary for its own development. Hence has it oft been given, when thou prayest enter into thine closet, or into thine self, and thine Father that seeth in secret shall reward thee openly. When thou attuned thine self to those vibrations, those necessary developments of thine own soul, the rewards are as that given—the end of that vibrated, for they are one. And while secularly or materially these may seem far afield, yet even unto the ends of the earth, even unto the beginning and end of time, the vibration, the truth of those forces of the creative energy are one, and—attuned—these bring those of the same attunement, for *all* are of *one spirit,* and the [different] variations are those creations as sparks are of that which set same in motion, for all are a portion of that first Creative Energy—God. [Author's italics]
2842-2

It could well be that here we find a clue to Cayce's statement that "The soul seeks consciousness as a diversion from the real," (3744-3) for we really do not want to know the future—or the past. We seek the vibrations we like, not knowing that they are attractive because of the lessons we can learn from them. "The blind leads the blind" then comes to have a much more personal meaning than we may have thought.

One may wonder about how the emotions relate to vibration, for surely we all know our emotions as vibratory forces. The correspondence between the two is indicated in the accompanying chart, which includes material drawn from a study of the Revelation. Here the symbols of the calf, man, lion and eagle are related to what are sometimes called the lower endocrine centers. But note also that earth, water, fire and air are correlated with the same centers. That these centers also relate to the emotions is usually accepted, for they are considered to apply to the lower natures of man, which the Revelation study identifies as the drives for sustenance (associated with the force focused in the gonads), propagation (lyden), preservation (solar plexus) and gratification (thymus). See chart on next page.

Perhaps we should consider these centers and the related emotions in the light of the evolution of the forces which are in matter, rather than simply stating that they are necessarily "lower" forces. Remember, these forces became a part of man when of his own free will he took on the animal natures. Consider the proposition that since man took on these (lower?) natures, he has a responsibility for their evolution while he is involved with them, for they too are forces that became, somehow, involved in the earth plane.[32] If we think about them as "forces which became involved in matter," then it is possible that they are here to serve us, to help us deal with our projection into matter; if this is so, it would seem to contradict the idea that they are to be shunned as merely "lower" natures. Seemingly they are "animal" natures; yet, since man took them on and became as one of the animals (*Homo sapiens*), does he not have an obligation to them? They are of that earth, for they are involved in the elements earth, water, fire and air—and so are we.

To view this proposition from another angle, remember that we become aware of these forces through the colors red, orange, yellow and green. If, in fact, green indicates change and is an evolutionary force within us, then it is no doubt accompanied by a responsibility to such forces as we are inclined to term "lower."

---

[32]One other example of a source that deals with "forces moving into and out of matter" is Velikovsky's *Worlds in Collision*. Regardless of how one views this man and his works, his illustration of the "forces" in evolution is quite clear.

COLOR	GLAND	PLANET	ANCIENT ELEMENT	BEAST	LORD'S PRAYER	CHURCH	OPENING OF SEAL
Violet	Pituitary	Jupiter			Heaven	Laodicea	Silence
Indigo	Pineal	Mercury			Name	Philadelphia	Upheavals (Earthquakes)
Blue	Thyroid	Uranus			Will	Sardis	Souls Slain
Green	Thymus	Venus	Air	Eagle	Evil	Thyatira	Pale Horse
Yellow	Solar Plexus	Mars	Fire	Lion	Debts	Pergamos	Red Horse
Orange	Lyden	Neptune	Water	Man	Temptation	Smyrna	Black Horse
Red	Gonads	Saturn	Earth	Calf	Bread	Ephesus	White Horse

Judgment

One of the most fascinating concepts to arise from a study of vibration is an unusual perspective of judgment of one another. We receive knowledge of each other through our five senses, correlate ideas received in this way with what we already know (our memories) and come up with concepts of one another. These concepts are really predicates for responses of one kind or another; hence we like some people and dislike others. In every case, though, it is *our* concept that we are reacting to, rather than someone else's.

Thus, when we judge another, it is *our* concept we have judged, and not the other person at all! In this light, Jesus' statement, "For with what judgment ye judge, ye shall be judged," (Matt. 7:2) becomes very, very personal—*we* have judged ourselves. In the same way, what we think of as condemnation of another is really self-condemnation. In fact, then we can never judge nor condemn anyone for anything, neither can we *blame* another, for in doing so we are condemning only ourselves; yet Jesus said we were forgiven already. (When are we going to pay attention to what that Man said?)

Evolution

Another interesting facet of our study lies in a consideration of the three spiritual principles (spirit, idea and purpose) and how they relate to man's evolution. Remember that these three principles are necessary for the manifestation of any atom, and thus they are present in every atom and every cell in the human body. Since man is evolving through the earth plane and thus through its four elements (earth, water, fire and air), we can see that there are twelve aspects to this development, for each of the three spiritual principles must evolve through each of the four elements to reach a full manifestation.

The importance of the number twelve, which is considered by many sources to have mystical significance, is reflected in the Old Testament. The readings tell us that the history of man from Noah to Abraham represents his physical development and his history from Abraham to Jesus is a picture of his mental development. The twelve sons of Jacob, then, could well be symbolic of the mental activities involved in using the four earthly elements in conjunction with the three principles of manifestation. It is almost as if the symbolism of our evolution necessitated that the sons of Jacob (which can be taken to represent the entire human race) be twelve in number:

3 principles (spirit, idea, purpose)
x4 elements (earth, water, fire, air)
$$\overline{}$$
12 sons

From this there follows 144, the square of 12, because the evolutionary force represented by each son must in turn evolve through each of the others before there could be full realization (mentally, that is) of the development of the forces, or separated vibrations. Thus man's mental evolution can be represented in the two equations $3 \times 4 = 12$ and $12 \times 12 = 144$.

There is an intriguing correlation between this evolutionary process and Einstein's formula $E = mc^2$. Of course, c stands for the speed of light, which can be equated with understanding, so that c^2 would represent complete understanding. To make our comparison easier, let us write our equations in a slightly different form:

3×4 (energy)=12 (manifestation) evolving through the forces (represented mathematically as 12^2) to reach full understanding; or
3×4 (energy)=12 (manifestation) c^2 (again, full understanding)

These equations describe the process by which each atom (or cell) in the body evolves through each element in order to develop complete knowledge of itself.

So that the material in the above paragraphs may not seem too far-fetched, consider this:

Spirit is the life-giving force in every condition, whether of mental or material action. Whatever force is acted upon has its attributes, the same as we find in all life-producing element. Whenever the element reaches that stage where it, the element, is able to give or reproduce self, we see the manifestation of the spirit force, modified by that element's own attributes, even from the lowest form of life to the highest. When we have the physical body of the lord of creation, man, we find all such conditions manifest through that body; the mind behind that element that directs and makes man the master of the condition, situation, or creation.

900-19

In relation to Jacob (man) and his sons, this development might be shown as follows:

1 Son	1 Son	1 Son	1 Son	
(Spirit x Earth) +	(Spirit x Water) +	(Spirit x Fire) +	(Spirit x Air)	= 4 Sons
(Idea x Earth) +	(Idea x Water) +	(Idea x Fire) +	(Idea x Air)	= 4 Sons
(Purpose x Earth) +	(Purpose x Water) +	(Purpose x Fire) +	(Purpose x Air)	= 4 Sons
				12 Sons

Then, since the force represented by each son must also move through each of the others, we of necessity have the equation $12 \times 12 = 144$ as a symbol of the entire human evolutionary process. Thus we have discovered a logical basis for 144,000 (1,000 was used to signify a large, indefinite number) being given in the Revelation as the symbolic number of perfected souls, those that have passed through every stage of evolution.

The Senses

There seems to be something magical about the number 12.[33] It has intrigued people since time immemorial, and perhaps quite rightly so, as we may discover by looking at it from a different angle. Ask anyone (or yourself) how many senses man has and invariably the answer you receive will be five. We all know what our five senses are; but do we? Is it not possible that this is a misconception, a shadow? Remember, what we call our five senses are really nothing but mechanical devices by which we perceive the essences of a vibration. If this is true, one may well ask what the five senses are a shadow of, what the real essence behind them is.

---

[33]See Immanuel Kant's "In All Theoretical Sciences of Reason Synthetical Judgments a Priori Are Contained as Principles," wherein he discourses about the "intuition" necessary to recognize the significance of the equation $5 + 7 = 12$. His discourse becomes much more meaningful when we consider that it is by reason of the seven angels that we "intuit" a meaning not deducible from mentally recallable concepts. Kant seems to address this problem in "The Universal Problem of Pure Reason." (It also may be interesting to speculate as to just why he chose these particular numbers [5 and 7] to make his point, since the two are clearly involved in all our intuitive processes. Our intuitions can rightly be called messages from the angels of the seven churches mentioned in the Revelation.)

It may well be that the five senses, as we know them, are just what they seem to be, necessary mechanical devices that are a part of the bodily functioning. Perhaps we have been under a misconception all along, our misconception being the shadow. Yet all may not be lost, for is it not by way of its shadow that we may come to know anything real at all? Once we look upon our five senses as shadows we may begin to wonder about them, to question whether we in fact have any senses at all.

Again, the answer may be found in the Cayce readings, if we can but accept it. If we can, we may also find the reason for the magic in the number 12, for it is through our five physical senses that we can come to know our real ones, and, if Cayce is right, they are seven in number. The five plus seven make twelve. Let us consider the following:

> Hence we find, as the churches are named, they are as the forces that are known as the senses, that must be spiritualized by the will of the individual made one in the very activities in a material world.
>
> 281-16

This passage is really a Pandora's box, as we will discover if we look into it. Cayce was speaking of the churches, as named in the book of Revelation. The readings tell us that the churches represent "bodies of activities" (281-16) within us, and these activities are related to those of the glandular forces, which in turn are related to the planetary forces.

For our purpose, the key words in the above quotation may be "the forces that are known as the senses." Now, who knows these forces to be the senses? Has anyone told us this before, and would we believe it if anybody did? Is it possible for us to figure this concept out so as to prove or disprove it? Whether we can do so or not may well be beside the point, for we may find that gaining some understanding of the "forces . . . as the senses" may help us to comprehend the rest of the quotation.

Consider again what we have discovered about how our "tree" develops and how the forces themselves "sense" our choices and use this information as a predicate for bringing to us the results that may be needed to fulfill those choices. It may well be the perceiving of those things that we *need* as our bread (the things that can be used to aid our development) requires a much higher sense than we ourselves have knowledge of; could this be the sensing that the above passage is talking about? Certainly the messages (in the Revelation) were to the "angels" of the churches, and thus to an intelligence greater than ours. And again, if an angel is a messenger of God, surely the messenger would carry to God information about what it is sensing. Thus God would know our innermost thoughts, perhaps even before we do. When we in turn sense the results of our choices (and when we realize the *purposes* of the results), we make use of the message brought to us by that angel. The activities of the churches, then, are our real sensing, and thus are a *process*, just like those of the bodily mechanical devices that we call our five senses—a shadow, if you please, of the real. But the inner sensing is through seven senses and the outer through five, which together make twelve. Herein lies the magic of the number 12, for by our sensing, inner and outer, we communicate with God! Once we have grasped this concept, the rest of the quotation falls easily into place.[34]

Summary

In this chapter we have investigated some of the ramifications of our study of vibration. Obviously, we have touched upon but a sampling of the many diverse phenomena that can be viewed with greater clarity once we have an understanding of vibration; indeed, it is a basic premise of this treatise that vibration is part and parcel of every atom in the manifested universe, and thus of every facet of life. The main points we considered in this chapter are as follows:

1. By drawing upon the vibrations we receive through all of our five senses, we arrive at a vibratory composite, which we use to locate ourselves in time and space. The normal tendency of the conscious mind is to focus on the external stimuli that evoke specific reactions in us; but if we could move away from this and tune in to the appropriate vibratory composite, we would be able to become aware of what is happening at any place and any time, and thus we would experience telepathy and/or clairvoyance. Through proper attunement we could become open to communication with other life forms or with those who have passed through the barrier we know as physical death.

---

[34]We might mention here that the reasoning presented in this section could help us to understand more completely the twelve sons of Jacob.

Like radios, we receive that to which we are attuned. And since each of us attunes his mind to his desires, we attract to ourselves the vibrations that we want to experience. Evaluating the results of these experiences leads us to seek those vibrations that can provide the lessons needed for our soul growth.

2. We all experience the emotions as vibratory forces. There is a correspondence between them and the four earthly elements, the four beasts mentioned in the Revelation, and the four "lower" endocrine centers; and because of this we might be inclined to ignore the emotions as being merely parts of man's "animal" nature. But man took on the emotions when he chose to project into matter and assume a body of flesh, and therefore he has a responsibility for their evolution. Meeting this responsibility by using these forces in our development through the physical would seem to be a more appropriate reaction than just shunning them as lower natures.

3. We receive vibrations from other people, correlate them with our memories, and arrive at concepts of one another. These concepts serve as the basis of our reactions to others, determining whether we like them or not. But it is *our concept* that we are reacting to and judging, rather than the other person. Thus when we condemn someone else we are really condemning ourselves; or, as Jesus said, "For with what judgment ye judge, ye shall be judged." (Matt. 7:2)

4. Because the three principles of spirit, idea and purpose underlie all physical manifestation, they are present in every atom in the human body. Man is evolving through the earth plane and thus through its four elements—earth, water, fire and air. There are, therefore, twelve evolutionary forces at work, for each spiritual principle must evolve to full manifestation through each of the elements. But, since each of these forces must in turn evolve through each of the others, we can see that 144 (12 x 12) is the number that best expresses the process whereby each atom in the body develops through each element to reach full understanding of itself. These concepts are symbolized in the Bible (in Jacob's sons, which can be taken to represent the entire human race in evolution, and in the 144,000 fully evolved souls mentioned in the Revelation), and they correlate well with the formula $E=mc^2$, where c^2—the square of the speed of *light*—can have the meaning of complete understanding.

5. Though we commonly think of ourselves as having five senses, the Edgar Cayce readings indicate that there are actually seven "forces that are known to the senses." (281-16) Could it be that the five physical senses are merely the shadow of the seven inner ones? It surely seems that some forms of sensing—for example, those in which the things needed for our soul growth are perceived, and those which reveal to us the purposes of the results of our choices—require much more than the mechanical devices we generally think of as our senses. If our five physical senses are in fact the reflection of seven inner ones, and if the seven plus the five are the means through which we communicate with our God, can it be any wonder that from very early times man has felt that there is something magical about 12, the sum of these two numbers?

Do not the above ideas show each of us to be a Pandora's box, full of strange and mysterious things that can lead us astray unless we learn to live according to the Lord's Prayer? And when we do come to live in this way, are we not still a Pandora's box, for do we not then have the hope that we can experience the miraculous? Perhaps we will find that, when we learn to surrender our will to the Father, the box that contains our potentials has grown into the city four-square mentioned in the Revelation—and it is of pure gold!

APPENDIX

Of the many Edgar Cayce readings that have been drawn upon in the formulation of the concepts put forth in this study, the following have been most important. Because of their great relevance to the subject of vibration as a whole, they are presented here in their entirety.

READINGS

Mrs. Cayce: You will have before you the Norfolk Study Group #1, members of which are preent in this room, and their studies on Day and Night. You will give at this time such guidance as will aid them in understanding this subject that it may be adequately presented for those who may study it. You will answer the questions which will be asked relating to it.

Mr. Cayce: Yes, we have the group as gathered here, as a group, as individuals.

As to the study of that being considered by the group at this time, it is the time or period—as given—when there should be a self-analysis of that each holds not only as an individual ideal and as a group ideal, but as to what is the belief upon the varied subjects that may be now presented from time to time. And when this decision is reached, how does each react to that each professes to believe?

For, as presented, what one believes alone is not sufficient; but what one does about that one believes either makes for advancement or growth, or retardment. For, in acting in the material plane may one do in all good conscience that one may develop in the line of thought set in motion by activities.

The first questions or subjects presented begin with the Beginning, as recorded in the accepted text or word of faith in the accepted Christian world. Then, the subject is *Night and Day*, or *Day and Night*.

In or from the material standpoint, night and day in the material world are only relative. For, were one to view the earth from an outer sphere there would be only varied shades; or *relatively* there would be night and day, from the position of the earth in its journey about the source of light. And, as given, these conditions that exist in the material plane are but shadows of the truths in the mental and spiritual plane.

Hence we find, as given, that first there was for matter, that gathered in a directed plane of activity called the earth, the separation of light and darkness.

Hence these, then, are figures of that from the spiritual plane termed in the mental world as the good and evil; or in the spiritual as facing the light and the dark, or facing the source of light—which, to the mind of those that seek to know His biddings, is the voice, the word, the life, the light, that comes in the hearts, minds, souls, of each to awaken them, as individuals, to their relationships with the source of light.

Again, in the figurative sense, we find that light and darkness, day and night, are represented by that termed as periods of growth and the periods of rest or recuperation, through the activities of other influences in those forces or sources of activity condensed in form to be called matter, no matter what plane this may be acting from or upon.

This would be the line of thought then, with each individual in the group answering to self that presented for consideration in this study. Ready for questions.

Q-1. [585]: Was it the Master's touch, the Master's voice, which I felt and heard one afternoon two winters ago?

A-1. As has been given.

Q-2. [288]: Is night the shadow of the original sin, or significant of man's seeking after knowledge which separated him from the light? and is that why children instinctively fear the dark?

A-2. It is both! Now this is leaving self to study some! For, it is both; but figure it out!

Q-3. [933]: Please explain why during the study of day and night, Eve has stood out so plainly and also Mark 14, Daniel 12.

A-3. Each here in their respective sphere of activity, Eve in hers. Daniel in recording the vision, or with the viewing of the wrestling between the forces of darkness and the forces of light. And that referred to in Mark as the source of light, the source of night. Each in his respective sphere presenting to a seeking mind a phase of the study. Hence each may be used as their shadow, or as their contribution to the study of the thought or lesson being presented.

Q-4. [560]: Was Jesus, the Christ, ever Job in the physical body? May this information be given?

A-4. No. Not ever in the physical body the Jesus. For, as the sons of God came together to reason, as recorded by Job, who recorded same? The Son of man! Melchizedek wrote Job!

Q-5. Was the experience I had in meditation in connection with the study of night and day? The words, "alpha and omega, the beginning and the ending. Thus saith the Lord." Please explain.

A-5. Compare this with that written in Isaiah, as to how the Lord, the God, is the beginning and the end of that brought into material manifestation, or into that known by man as the plane or dimension from which man reasons in the finite. Then there will be to the body the correct conception of that meant. "I am alpha and omega, beginning and the end." That God, the Father, the Spirit, the Ohm, is the influencing

110

force of every activity is not wholly sufficient unto man's salvation, in that he is a free-will being. As intimated that alpha beginning, omega ending. For, the confirmation, the segregation, the separation, the building, the adding to it, is necessary—in relation to those activities that lie between—for man's building to the beginning and the end.

Q-6. [303]: *Please explain to me the affirmation given in this lesson, that I may be able to apply it in my activities better.*

A-6. As in the material life there is the day, in which the activities of the body are put in motion to supply the material things of the earth, and—as shown—such materials add to the abilities of the body to carry on in its daily activities, through the sustenance gained by the attitudes of self in the daily activity; so it is seen in the same association and connection that the night becomes the period of meditation, rest, associations of those ideas through the activities of the day; which are the gift not of self, not of self's abilities, but from the source from which mercies, truth, love, knowledge, understanding, arise. So is given, "May Thy mercies guide" in the understanding, that the concepts of that presented in *Day and Night, Night and Day,* may be builded in self in such a manner as to make for the glorifying *in* the activities of self day *and* night to the glory of Him that *is* the Maker, the Giver, the Father of light.

Q-7. [413]: *Please give me the significance of the dream I had the night of Sept. 26th at which time I saw the Master.*

A-7. As there has been in self that seeking more and more for the material confirmation of the thought, the intent and the purpose of self's activities, so in that given, that seen, is a confirmation of that purpose, that thought, that activity.

Hence, rather than bring fears on the part of self, or anxiety as respecting those visioned in same, rather know that self is being led by Him who *is* the Guide, the Giver, the Promise to all mankind.

Q-8. *Compilers: Please give some suggestions for outlines.*

A-8. In the beginning, as presented, first the approach will be in the introduction from the *material* basis of presentation. Then, in the latter portion of introduction, both the mental and spiritual presentation.

Then, that which may be given under each heading as the contribution from those that study this as given.

Q-9. *Please explain the part of the affirmation, "Day unto day uttereth speech, night unto night sheweth knowledge."*

A-10. *This* is to be applied in each *individual* experience. For, day unto day uttereth speech, whether from the material, the mental or the spiritual aspect; as does night show forth in the varied applications the same as given of life; for it *is* alpha and omega. For, this must be determined, as to the basis of the hope that is within each:

Did, is, was, God, the Father, worshiped by each, honored by those that love His name; dishonored by those who seek their own rather than His biddings? Is He, was He, the Creator of all things? Or came it, the earth, the heavens, the day, the night, into being by chance?

111

Mrs. Cayce: You will give at this time an interpretation of the Book of Revelation as recorded in the King James version of the Bible, explaining the general plan and theme, the significance of the Book, and give such explanations of the symbols used as will make this book of personal value to those present seeking to awaken and develop the inner life. You will then answer the questions which will be asked regarding various parts of this Book.

Mr. Cayce: Yes, we have the text written in the Revelation, as recorded in the King James version of same.

In making this worthwhile in the experience of individuals who are seeking for the light, for the revelation that may be theirs as promised in the promises of same, it would be well that there be considered first the conditions which surrounded the writer, the apostle, the beloved, the last of those chosen; writing to a persecuted people, many despairing, many fallen away, yet, many seeking to hold to that which had been delivered to them through the efforts and activities of those upon whom the spirit had fallen by the very indwelling and the manifestations that had become the common knowledge of all.

Remember, then, that Peter—chosen as the rock, chosen to open the doors of that known today as the church—had said to this companion, "I will endeavor to keep thee in remembrance; even after my demise I will return to you." [II Peter 1:15]

The beloved, then, was banished to the isle, and was in meditation, in prayer, in communion with those saints who were in that position to see, to comprehend the greater needs of those that would carry on.

And, as given in the beginning, "I was in the Spirit on the Lord's day, and beheld, and heard, and saw, and was told to *write*."

Why, then, ye ask now, was this written (this vision) in such a manner that is hard to be interpreted, save in the experience of every soul who seeks to know, to walk in, a closer communion with Him?

For the visions, the experiences, the names, the churches, the places, the dragons, the cities, all are but emblems of those forces that may war within the individual in its journey through the material, or from the entering into the material manifestation to the entering into the glory, or the awakening in the spirit, in the interbetween, in the borderland, in the shadow.

Hence we find, as the churches are named, they are as the forces that are known as the senses, that must be spiritualized by the will of the individual made one in the very activities in a material world.

And the elders and the Lamb are the emblems, are the shadows of those acceptances or rejections that are made in the experiences of the individual.

As we find, in the various manners and forms that are presented as the vision or visions proceed, every force that is manifest is of one source; but the soul, the will of the individual, either makes such into a coordinating

112

or cooperating influence in bringing about more and more manifestations in the material world of those experiences that are seen from the spiritual conditions, or the opposite.

Why, then, is it presented, ye ask, in the form of symbols? Why is there used those varied activities? These are for those that were, or will be, or may become, through the seeking, those initiated into an understanding of the glories that may be theirs, if they will but put into work, into activity, that they know in the present.

In seeking, then, do individuals find from the beginning that there is presented, in every line, in every form, that good and bad (as termed) that arises from their activity, in what they do about that knowledge they have respecting the law, the love, the mercy, the understanding of the wherefore of the Lamb's advent into the world that they, through His ensample set, may present themselves before that throne even as He, becoming—as given—heirs, joint heirs with Him, as the sons of God, to that *everlasting* glory that may be had in Him.

Then, seek to know to what self is lacking, even as given in the first four chapters (as divided in the present).

What is lacking in self? Are ye cold? Are ye hot? Have ye been negligent of the knowledge that is thine? Are ye stiff-necked? Are ye adulterous in thought, in act, in the very glories that are thine?

Then, again—may ye not have had through the varied experiences those presentations before the throne, even as the elders twenty and four that are represented by the figures within thine own head, that which is shown in the physical forces of self? Has it not been given to thee, or has not the message come as the rider of the pale, the black, the white, or the red horses that are the figures of the messages that have come to thee in thine varied experiences? Or, art thou among the figures represented in the Babylon, or in the rivers of blood, or in the trees of life?

These we see, then, represent *self*; self's body-physical, self's body-mental, self's body-spiritual; with the attributes of the body-physical, attributes of the body-mental, attributes of the body-spiritual, and they are *one* in thee—even as the Father, the Son and the Holy Spirit is one in Him.

Then, doest thou seek to enter into the glories of the Father? Whosoever will may come, may take of the water of life freely—even as flows from the throne of the Lamb. For, the very leaves of the trees are for the healing of the nations, and—if ye will accept—the blood cleanses from all unrighteousness. How? From what? Saves self from what? To what are ye called? To know that only from the falling away of self may ye be saved. Unto the glorifying of self in Him may ye be saved.

Then, whosoever will, come!

Ready for questions:

Q-1. Please interpret the fall of Babylon as referred to in the 14th, 17th, and 18th chapters of Revelation.

A-1. Babylon represented the individual; those periods through which every soul passes in its delving into the varied mysteries that are the experiences of the carnal-mental, the spiritual-mental forces of the body; and, as viewed from that presented, may come to the knowledge only through the *cleansing* that is shown must come to those that would be saved from the destructions that are given there.

Q-2. What did the angel mean when he said: "I will tell thee the mystery of the woman, and of the beast that carrieth her"?

A-2. That which is understood by those that follow in the way of the Lamb, that come to know how man separates himself through the desires to become as the procreator in the beasts; which made the necessity of the shedding of blood for redemption, for it brought sin *in* the shedding— and only through same may there be the fulfilling; and, as given, the heavens and the earth may pass, but His law, His love, His mercy, His grace, endureth for those who *will* seek to know His will.

Q-3. Where are the dead until Christ comes? Do they go direct to Him when they die?

A-3. As visioned by the beloved, there are those of the saints making intercession always before the throne for those that are passing in and out of the interbetween; even as He, the Christ, is ever in the consciousness of those that are redeemed in Him.

The passing in, the passing out, is as but the summer, the fall, the spring; the birth into the interim, the birth into the material.

Q-4. In what form does the anti-Christ come, spoken of in Revelation?

A-4. In the spirit of that opposed to the spirit of truth. The fruits of the spirit of the Christ are love, joy, obedience, long-suffering, brotherly love, kindness. Against such there is no law. The spirit of hate, the anti-Christ, is contention, strife, fault-finding, lovers of self, lovers of praise. Those are the anti-Christ, and take possession of groups, masses, and show themselves even in the lives of men.

Q-5. Will we be punished by fire and brimstone?

A-5. That as builded by self; as those emblematical influences are shown through the experiences of the beloved in that builded, that created. For, each soul is a portion of creation—and builds that in a portion of its experience that it, through its physical-mental or spiritual-mental, has builded for itself. And each entity's heaven or hell must, through *some* experience, be that which it has builded for itself.

Is thy hell one that is filled with fire or brimstone? But know, each and every soul is tried so as by fire; purified, purged; for He, though He were the Son, learned obedience through the things which He suffered. Ye also are known even as ye do, and have done.

Q-6. Is this the period of the great tribulation spoken of in Revelation, or just the beginning, and if so just how can we help ourselves and others to walk more closely with God?

A-6. The great tribulation and periods of tribulation, as given, are the experiences of every soul, every entity. They arise from influences created by man through activity in the sphere of any sojourn. Man may become, with the people of the universe, ruler of any of the various spheres through which the soul passes in its experiences. Hence, as the

114

cycles pass, as the cycles are passing, when there *is* come a time, a period of readjusting in the spheres (as well as in the little earth, the little soul)—seek, then, as known, to present self spotless before that throne; even as *all* are commanded to be circumspect, in thought, in act, to that which is held by self as that necessary for the closer walk with Him. In that manner only may each atom (as man is an atom, or corpuscle, in the body of the Father) become a helpmeet with Him in bringing that to pass that all may be one with Him.

Q-7. *What is meant by the four beasts?* ·

A-7. As given, the four destructive influences that make the greater desire for the carnal forces, that rise as the beasts within self to destroy. Even as man, in his desire to make for companionship, brought those elements within self's own experience. These must be met. Even as the dragon represents the one that separated self so far as to fight with, to destroy with, those that would make of themselves a kingdom of their own.

Q-8. *What is meant by "a new heaven and a new earth"?*

A-8. Former things have passed away, when there is beheld within self that the whole will of the Creator, the Father, the place of abode, the forces within and without, make for the *new* heaven, the *new* earth.

We are through.   281-16

Mrs. Cayce: You will have before you the Glad Helpers, members of which are present here. You will continue with answering questions which will be presented on Revelation.

Mr. Cayce: Yes, we have the Glad Helpers Group, as a group, as individuals; and the study that has been made by same on Revelation. In adding to *some* of those things as have been applied, let each consider how and why that such application would be made by the beloved in a message of the nature and character. First, the body of the Christ represented to the world a channel, a door, a mediation to the Father. Hence this then may become as the study of self in its relationship to the material world, the mental world, the spiritual world. And this is the manner that has been presented as the way through which each individual would make application of same, of the life of the Christ in his or her own experience.

Q-1. *Are we correct in interpreting the seven churches as symbols of seven spiritual centers in the physical body?*

A-1. Correct.

Q-2. *Do we have these correctly placed? As each is called, comment on each in relation to an individual's development and experiences in connection with these centers. Gonads—Ephesus; Lyden—Smyrna; Solar Plexus—Pergamos; Thymus—Thyatira; Thyroid—Sardis; Pineal—Philadelphia; Pituitary—Laodicea.*

A-2. Rather than the commenting, it is well that these are correctly placed, but each individual's *experience* in the application of that gained by each in his or her experience will be different. To give an

115

interpretation that the opening or activity through a certain center raises or means or applies this or that, then would become rote. But know the way, then each may apply same as his or her environment, ability, experience, gives the opportunity. For know, in all and through all, the activity of self is only as a channel—and God giveth the understanding, the increase, to such; and in the manner as is best fitted for the individual. It is not then as a formula, that there are to be certain activities and certain results. These are true in the sense that they each represent or present the opportunity for the opening to the understanding of the individual, but the application is as to the individual. For, as has been given, man is free-willed. And only when this is entirely given, and actively given, to the will of the Father may it be even as the life of the Christ.

Q-3. *Which is the highest gland in the body—the pineal or the pituitary?*
A-3. The pituitary!

Q-4. *Are we correct in interpreting the twenty-four elders as the twenty-four cranial nerves of the head especially related to the five senses?*
A-4. Correct.

Q-5. *Is the frequent reference to the throne indicating the head in which are found the higher gland centers?*
A-5. Correct.

Q-6. *Are we correct in interpreting the four beasts as the four fundamental physical natures (desires) of man which must be overcome? Give us more light on each of these.*
A-6. Correct.

In all of these, let this be understood: These are symbolized; they are as in these representing the elemental forces—as the body is of the earth, is of the elements. For as has so oft been given, and as may be found in man, every element or every influence that is outside of man is found in the *living* man—not a dead one but a *living* man! For the *living* force is that *of* which all that is *was* brought into being. Hence all the influences, all the forces, all the activities are in that. And in man, man's experience, there never has been, never will be found in material activity an instrument, an action, that is not shown as a replica or expression or manifestation of that in a living man; whether it be in this, that or the other of the forces of nature, of activity. For when such is active, unless found in man—or an answer to something within, it would not be cognizable by man.

Q-7. *Do we have these four beasts placed correctly in relation to the centers in the body and the ancient elementals? Air—Eagle—Thymus?*
A-7. These are *relatively*, yes. Relatively correct.

Q-8. *Fire—Lion—Solar Plexus?*
A-8. Correct.

Q-9. *Water—Man—Lyden?*
A-9. Yes.

Q-10. *Earth—Calf—Gonads?*
A-10. Yes.

Q-11. *Is the book with the seven seals the human body with the seven spiritual centers?*

A-11. This is correct.

Q-12. Do we have the opening of the seals correctly placed in our chart? As each is called, give advice that will help us in properly opening these centers.

A-12. [Interrupting] First, let's give as this: Do not attempt to open any of the centers of the book until self has been tried in the balance of self's own conscious relationship to the Creative Forces and not found wanting by the spiritual answer in self to that rather as is seen in the manner in which the book itself becomes as that in the whole body which may be assimilated by the body, when taken properly. In these then there has been set as ye have in thine outline. These are well. *Do not* misuse them!

Q-13. Gonads—White Horse?

A-13. Yes.

Q-14. Lyden—Black Horse?

A-14. Yes.

Q-15. Solar Plexus—Red Horse?

A-15. Yes.

Q-16. Thymus—Pale Horse?

A-16. Yes.

For a reference to these, let each in your study of these, as in relation to the centers themselves, consider the effect of the color itself upon thine own body as ye attempt to apply same by either concentration, dedication or meditating upon these. For as has been given, color is but vibration. Vibration is movement. Movement is activity of a positive and negative force. Is the activity of self as in relationship to these then positive? Proceed.

Q-17. Thyroid—Souls slain for Word of God?

A-17. Correct.

Q-18. What color here?

A-18. Gray.

Q-19. Pineal—Upheavals?

A-19. Correct, but this would have to be *relatively* so. For these are at those periods when, in the colors that these arise to—which are of the purple, they become rather such that there *must* be the *disseminating* or the giving away of the egoism of self. Consider as an example in thy study of same, the servant Moses. For these become as may be found even for and from that record as ye have, the stumbling block at Meribah.

Q-20. Pituitary—Silence?

A-20. Silence, golden; the forces upon which the greater expression has been set of all the influences of might and power as may be seen in man's experience—*Silence* if ye would hear the Voice of thy Maker!

Q-21. Do the planets as placed in our chart have proper relation and significance? Pituitary—Jupiter; Pineal—Mercury; Thyroid—Uranus; Thymus—Venus; Solar Plexus—Mars; Lyden—Neptune; Gonads—Saturn?

A-21. These are very well done. These vary, to be sure, according to the variation of an *experience*. For these are the variable forces in the very nature of man himself, for he partakes of all and from all the influences and forces. For remember as has been given, it is not that the planets rule the man; rather has man, as man of God, ruled the planets! For he's a portion of same.

Then, these are as we have given; only relative. Relatively, these are correct. At times these are represented by others. It is here the application of these influences in the experience of the individual rather than there being set, as it were, a blanket to cover each and every individual.

Q-22. *Does the outline of the Lord's Prayer as placed on our chart have any bearing on the opening of the centers?*

A-22. Here is indicated the manner in which it was given as to the purpose for which it was given; not as an *only* way but as a way that would answer for those that sought to be—as others—seekers for *a* way, *an* understanding, to the relationships to the Creative Forces. It bears in relationships to this, then, the proper place.

Q-23. *Pituitary—Heaven?*

A-23. Correct. In all of its activities these open, for the upward lift of the thoughts of man as in relationships to that which becomes—how has it been given?—"He is alpha, omega, the beginning and the end." Hence as we find in its relationships to man, it becomes then the beginnings, the endings, of all things.

Q-24. *Pineal—Name?*

A-24. Relatively, yes.

Q-25. *Thyroid—Will?*

A-25. Correct.

Q-26. *Thymus—Evil?*

A-26. Correct.

Q-27. *Solar Plexus—Debts?*

A-27. Yes.

Q-28. *Lyden—Temptation?*

A-28. Correct.

Q-29. *Gonads—Bread?*

A-29. Right.

Q-30. *How should the Lord's Prayer be used in this connection?*

A-30. As in feeling, as it were, the flow of the meanings of each portion of same throughout the body-physical. For as there is the response to the mental representations of all of these in the *mental* body, it may build into the physical body in the manner as He, thy Lord, thy brother, so well expressed in, "I have bread ye know not of."

Q-31. *What is meant by the seven lamps of fire burning before the throne, described as the seven spirits of God—Ch. 4:5?*

A-31. Those influences or forces which in their activity in the natures of man are without, that stand ever before the throne of grace—or God, to become the messengers, the aiders, the destructions of hindrances; as the ways between man's approach to—as was represented in the ways of dividing man's knowledge of or between—good and evil. Hence they work ever as those influences or forces that stand between, as it were; being the helpful influences that become as the powers of activity in the very nature or force of man.

Q-32. What is meant by the angels at the four corners of the earth as given in Ch. 7?

A-32. These are only as from the body-forces ever. There are those four influences or forces in the nature of man from his source; as in environment, heredity as of the earth and as of the mental and spiritual. These are as the four corners that become represented here as the very natures or forces to which all approaches to all these influences are made in the very nature of man.

Q-33. Are we correct in interpreting the 144,000 who were sealed as being spiritualized cellular structure of the twelve major divisions of the body?

A-33. Correct. And this is as of a man, and the name of same.

Q-34. Are the zodiacal divisions of the body proper and do they have any relation to this?

A-34. Only relatively. For this is as we have given again and again in reference to same; for as they have been set as the zodiacal signs, correct. As they have moved in their orb or their sphere about the earth, these have just recently passed and have become—as has been indicated—a very different nature to them.

Q-35. Is the multitude before the throne as described in Ch. 7 the rest of the cellular structure in process of spiritualization?

A-35. This is correct.

Q-36. Are we correct in interpreting the sounding of the seven angels as the experience during physical purification?

A-36. Correct.

We are through for the present.   281-29

Mrs. Cayce: You will have before you the Glad Helpers of the Association for Research and Enlightenment, Inc., members of which are present here; and their study of the Book of Revelation together with the information given them through this channel on Oct. 26, 1936, and Oct. 28, 1936, in connection with this study. You will answer the questions regarding this study which will be asked.

Mr. Cayce: Yes, we have the work of the Glad Helpers, together with their study of Revelation, and the information which has been given respecting same. In the beginning again we would give this, that it may be clarified in the minds of those who seek to have the interpretation of *the* Revelation in their own experience:

Know first that the knowledge of God is a growing thing, for ye grow in grace, in knowledge, in understanding *as* ye apply that ye KNOW. But remember, as has been given by Him, to know to do good and do it not is sin.

In the interpretation then of the Revelation as given by John in

Patmos: This was John's revelation of *his* experience, and interpreted in the individual by the application of the body of self as a pattern with the attributes physically, mentally, spiritually, in their respective spheres for thine *own* revelation.

For this to be practical, to be applicable in the experience of each soul, it must be an individual experience; and the varied experiences or activities of an entity in its relationship to the study of self are planned, builded, workable in the pattern as John has given in the Revelation.

Each attribute of the body, whether organ or functioning or the expression of same, becomes then in the experience of each soul as a seeker first. Seek and ye shall find, knock and it shall be opened unto you!

Then in thy study, for those who would become Glad Helpers, in the physical, in the moral, in the mental, in the spiritual life of each soul: Condemn no one. Love all. Do good. And ye may experience it all.

Ready for questions.

Q-1. Please discuss more fully the relation of colors to the seven major glandular centers. Do the colors vary for each center with different individuals, or may definite colors be associated with each center?

A-1. Both. For to each—remember, to study each of these in the light not only of what has just been given but that as is a practical experience in the material world; as is known, vibration is the essence or the basis of color. As color and vibration then become to the consciousness along the various centers in an individual's experience in meditation made aware, they come to mean definite experiences. Just as anger is red, or as something depressing is blue; yet in their shades, their tones, their activities, to each they begin with the use of same in the experience to mean those various stages. For instance, while red is anger, rosy to most souls means delight and joy—yet to others, as they are formed in their transmission from center to center, come to mean or to express what *manner* of joy; whether that as would arise from a material, a mental or a spiritual experience. Just as may be seen in the common interpretation of white, but with all manner of rays from same begins or comes to mean that above the aura of all in its vibration from the body and from the activity of the mental experience when the various centers are vibrating to color.

Q-2. If so, give color for: (1) Gonads (2) Lyden (3) Solar Plexus (4) Thymus (5) Thyroid (6) Pineal (7) Pituitary.

A-2. These come from the leaden, going on through to the highest—to that as is the halo. To each they become the various forces as active throughout, and will go in the regular order of the prism.

Q-3. What is the significance of the color of the four horses associated with four lower centers; pale horse for Thymus; red for Solar Plexus; black for Lyden; white for Gonads?

A-3. That comes as has just been given as the illustration of same from the *emotions* or physical forces that ride forth to their expression in the higher forces of the activity.

Q-4. Please explain what was meant in reading of Oct. 28, regarding the "relative" connection of Name in the Lord's Prayer with the Pineal gland.

A-4. This might occupy a whole period of several hours, if the full conclusion were to be given; but each must reach this. There is a Name to each soul. For He hath called His own *by name!* What name? All the names that may have been as a material experience through an earthly sojourn, or all the names that may have been through the experience of an entity in that environ or those relative associations of Venus, Mars, Jupiter, Uranus, Saturn, Sun, Moon, or what! Or a Name that is above *every* name!

Then as has been indicated this becomes relative, as is signified in the indication as given to the number, which is of John's own. But as has been given, every influence—you see—is *relative!* Hence the name is relative to that which is accomplished by the soul in its sojourn throughout its whole experience; whether in those environs about this individual sphere or another—this individual sphere meaning thine own sun, thine own planets with all of their attributes (does an earth mind comprehend such?) and is carried through with what is its *relative* force to that which has been or is the activity of the entity-soul (not a body now at all!) toward Constructive Force or God, or God's infinite force to that integral activity of the soul in its sojourn. Hence it becomes *relative.* And for the finite mind to say Jane, John, Joe, James or Jude would mean only as the *vibrations* of those bring the *relative* force or influence to which, through which an entity's sojourns have brought the concrete experience in any one given or definite period of activity!

Was one named John by chance? Was one named Joe or Llewellyn by chance? No; they are relative! While it may be truly in the material plane relative because you have a rich aunt by that name, or relative because an uncle might be named that—but these carry then the vibrations of same; and in the end the name is the sum total of what the soul-entity in all of its vibratory forces has borne toward the Creative Force itself.

Hence each soul has a definite influence upon the experiences through which it may be passing. This ye have illustrated in thine own secret organizations, in thy papal activities in the religious associations, and in each vibration. For when ye have set a vibration by the activity of thy *soul's* force, ye are then either in parallel, in direct accord, or in opposition to constructive force—whatever may be the position or activity of the soul in infinity. For ye *are* gods! But you are becoming devils or real gods!

Q-5. What was meant in the reading of Oct. 28, in connection with 144,000 who were sealed as being spiritualized cellular structure of the twelve major divisions of the body, when the reading gave, "Correct, and this is as of a man, and the name of same." Please explain.

A-5. Just as has been illustrated or given, as to the relative force of the vibratory forces of the individual; which is shown in an individual soul or entity by its name and its activity in all the influences or environs through which it passes in that which is a shadow in man (active, living) to those influences that are relative to the infinitive position of a soul's activity in a universe.

Q-6. In connection with the symbols of Revelation, what are the twelve major divisions of the body?

A-6. Those that are of the general construction and those that are of the keeping alive physical, and those that are in keeping with the influences to the mental, to the material, to the spiritual; and the illustrations are shown in the bodily forces that are opened for those activities in a material plane.

Q-7. What is meant by the symbol of the angel with the golden censer and incense described in Rev. 8:3-5?

A-7. As the influence is visualized in the experience of each soul by the name as implied in "angel," or the good that goes out from the individual soul in its relationships to the influences or forces about same, so is it called or given as the angel with the censer of the activities that emanate from each individual. And as has been given in other illustrations, that ye *are*—that of good—rises ever as an incense, sweet before the throne of mercy. Or to take the back track, as it were, and take the angel with the censer, with the incense that is before the image of a soul seeking to become one with the Creative Forces or God—that which has been kind, gentle, patient, merciful, long-suffering in self's experience during a day, rises before the throne of the mercy seat within self to that of an incense of satisfaction. Why? Hate, unkindness, harshness, all such become as base in thine own experience, and as usual one condemns self by saying, "Why can't I do this or that?" And, "What is the use?" Well—and the censer is broken!

Q-8. Do the seven angels described in Rev. 8-9 represent spiritual forces governing the various dimensional planes through which souls pass between incarnations on the earth? Please explain.

A-8. This is a very good interpretation. Yes. While this explanation becomes a portion of another group's study and activity in the lesson just being approached on *happiness*, it may be best explained in this; as to how this must indeed be interpreted in the experience of each soul, whether considered in a material plane in which there is found the real essence of happiness or that in the interim when ye are looked over, or when the promises become more and more as has been interpreted from that given by others—to be absent from the body-physical is to be present in the grace and glory and presence of divinity; or to be those influences that make for an activity in an influence without self.

Now ye are studying yourself! Do not confuse the interpretation with that outside of thyself, but happiness is love of something outside of self! It may never be obtained, may never be known by loving only things within self or self's own domain!

Then the expression that has been given by an entity in a sojourn in the earth becomes as a portion of that activity as has been given, "He hath given His angels charge concerning thee, lest at any time ye dash thy foot against a stone."

Hence we find that in the expression then of those interims where there are the guiding influences of that we have loved, we have love—for this becomes then very definite.

If ye have loved self-glory, if ye have loved the honor of the people more than those thoughts of the mental and spiritual and moral welfare, what manner of angels will direct thee between thy interims?

Think on the study then of self, in thy body—but let it all become as has been *so oft* given:

Study to show thyself approved unto God, the God in self, the God in thine own consciousness—that *is* creative in its essence: rightly divining and dividing the words of truth and light; keeping self unspotted from the world. And ye become lights to those that sit in darkness, to those that wander.

Though ye may be reviled, revile not again. Though ye may be spoken of harshly, smile—*smile!* For it is upon the river of life that smiles are made. Not grins! No Cheshire cat activities bring other than those that are of the earth, of such natures that create in the minds and the experiences those things that become repulsive. But the smile of understanding cheers on the hearts of those who are discouraged, who are disheartened.

It costs so little! It does thee so much good, and lifts the burdens of so many!

We are through for the present.   281-30

Mr. [900]: Now you have before you the book on subject matter, written by the body, Edgar Cayce, in the subconscious condition, in the hand of [900], present in this room. You will also have before you the outline of this book, written by the body, [900], also in the body, [900]'s hand, present in this room. You will answer questions, so as to clarify the book on subject matter [3744] to the mind of [900].

Mr. Cayce: Yes, we have the subject matter here, as transcribed and written. Also the explanation on subject matter as written by the body, [900]. We have in this subject matter many conditions that may be clarified by questions.

Ready for questions.

Q-1. Explain, "Mind is the factor that is in direct opposition to will."

A-1. We have many phases of mind. We have the mind of the spirit consciousness, of the physical subconscious, or soul. We have the mind of the physical body, through which any or all of these may manifest. The will is that active principle against which such manifestations respond. Hence it is in direct opposition to mind action. This, we find then, refers to the condition in the material world, will, see? The will in the spiritual plane, or spirit consciousness (not spirit entity) being the creation of that manifested in the earth plane. Hence the different conditions in will's manifesting and how will is in opposition to the mind force.

Q-2. Explain, "Mind is a factor as senses are of the mind, and as the soul and spirit are factors of the entity, one in all, all in one."

A-2. As has been given. These conditions, mind of the soul, mind of the

123

physical body, mind of the spiritual entity, are separated, that one may gain the knowledge of its action. As we have then in the mind of the spiritual entity, that mind wherein the entity (spiritual entity we are speaking of) manifests in the spiritual plane; the mind in the physical body [is] the subconscious, the conscious, through which the entity manifests in the physical world; one in all, all in one. In one, in the spiritual mind, acted upon by their attributes, principally will, for it is the factor in the physical world, in the spiritual world, for the action being that through which the manifestations of any factor are known. As we would have in this: Knowledge comes through the senses in the physical body to the conscious mind. The subconscious has the storing of the knowledge of given conditions; when the consciousness receives through the sense that knowledge, the will is the action against the incentives set forth.

Q-3. *Explain how the mind segregates, correlates, or divides the impressions to the portion needed to develop the entity, or physical force, toward the spark or infinite force, giving the life force to the body.*

A-3. In this, again we have the manifestations of physical conditions that may be manifest in a physical body, and conditions that may be manifest in the spiritual body. As we have in correlation of conditions that assist in the building, the developing, in the physical body, the entity, the inmost being, the expectancy of the physical body must be awakened before the body, through its tissue, its vital forces, can emanate the necessary building, or eliminating forces, of the physical body, to rebuild or develop properly. Hence the cause of death in the physical world. The lack of the consciousness of the indwelling spiritual force in the spiritual entity in a physical body. The breaking, the division, in the portions. Hence the disintegration of physical to the birth in the spiritual. As we have again in the physical the correlation of those elements necessary for the setting in motion of those vibrations to create the offspring, the developing begins with the separation of those elements in the physical body to create physical body, born into physical world. The knowledge of the spiritual forces begins the development through the awakening of the spiritual forces in the entity. Hence the birth into the spiritual world. Hence the necessity of the rebirth in and through such conditions, until the whole is made in the will of the Creator.

Q-4. *Explain what the divide between the soul and spiritual forces is. How manifest, and how we may study self to gain the approach to that divide.*

A-4. This is of the spiritual entity in its entirety. The superconscious is the divide, that oneness lying between the soul and the spirit force, within the spiritual entity. Not of earth forces at all, only awakened with the spiritual indwelling and acquired individually.

Q-5. *How may the individual think, study, and act to acquire this awakening?*

A-5. Study to show thyself approved unto Him, rightly dividing the words of truth, keeping self unspotted from the world, avoiding the appearance of evil, for as is given, those who would seek God must believe that He *is*, and a rewarder of those who would seek Him. That is, that the Creator has that oneness with the individual to make that oneness with Him. As is given in the conditions as manifest through those who would seek the oneness with God, for only those who have approached sufficient to make the mind of the physical, the mind of the soul, the mind of the spiritual, one with Him, may understand or gather that necessary to approach that understanding.

Q-6. Explain, "the only real life being that which in the material or physical plane is called psychic."

A-6. This we find has been given in explanation of psychic.

We are through for the present.   900-21

THE WORK OF EDGAR CAYCE TODAY

The Association for Research and Enlightenment, Inc. (A.R.E.®), is a membership organization founded by Edgar Cayce in 1931.

• 14,256 Cayce readings, the largest body of documented psychic information anywhere in the world, are housed in the A.R.E. Library/Conference Center in Virginia Beach, Virginia. These readings have been indexed under 10,000 different topics and are open to the public.

• An attractive package of membership benefits is available for modest yearly dues. Benefits include: a journal and newsletter; lessons for home study; a lending library through the mail, which offers collections of the actual readings as well as one of the world's best parapsychological book collections, names of doctors or health care professionals in your area.

• As an organization on the leading edge in exciting new fields, A.R.E. presents a selection of publications and seminars by prominent authorities in the fields covered, exploring such areas as parapsychology, dreams, meditation, world religions, holistic health, reincarnation and life after death, and personal growth.

• The unique path to personal growth outlined in the Cayce readings is developed through a worldwide program of study groups. These informal groups meet weekly in private homes.

• A.R.E. maintains a visitors' center where a bookstore, exhibits, classes, a movie, and audiovisual presentations introduce inquirers to concepts from the Cayce readings.

• A.R.E. conducts research into the helpfulness of both the medical and nonmedical readings, often giving members the opportunity to participate in the studies.

For more information and a color brochure, write or phone:

A.R.E., Dept. C., P.O. Box 595
Virginia Beach, VA 23451, (804) 428-3588